The Agnes & Muriel's Cafe

COOKBOOK

The *Agnes & Muriel's* Cafe
COOKBOOK

Glenn Powell

illustrations by *Daniel Gill*

LONGSTREET PRESS
Atlanta, Georgia

Published by LONGSTREET PRESS, INC.
2140 Newmarket Parkway
Suite 122
Marietta, Georgia 30067

Printed in the United States of America

1st printing, 2000

Library of Congress Catalog Number 00-105069

ISBN: 1-56352-621-2

Cover design by Burtch Hunter and Megan Wilson
Book design by Megan Wilson
Illustrations by Daniel Gill
Edited by Elizabeth McDonald

Table of Contents

Foreword v

Introduction vii

Acknowledgments ix

Just the Basics 1
On Recipes 3
On Equipment 7
On Ingredients 8
On Useful Techniques 11

Starters 13
Corn "Fritters" 15
Fried Asparagus 16
Salmon Croquettes 17
Stuffed Portobello Mushrooms 18
Baked Potato Soup 19
Roasted Elephant Garlic 20
Cucumber Dill Vichyssoise 22
Summer Gazpacho 23
Smoked Salmon Chowder 24
Crab Bisque 26

Salads 27
Michelle's Cabbage Slaw 29
Carmen Miranda Chicken Salad 30
Grilled Garlic Broccoli Salad 32
Peanut Pickled Beets 34
Watermelon Vidalia Salad 35
Grilled Lettuce Caesar Salad
    with Caesar Dressing 36
Balsamic Dressing 38
Green Goddess Dressing 39
Buttermilk Ranch Dressing 40

Entrées 41
Cracked Mustard Seed Chicken 43
BBQ Baby Back Ribs and Rib Rub 44
Grilled Pork Chops
    with Cinnamon Apple Fritters 46
Turkey Meatloaf 47
Louisiana BBQ Shrimp
    over Country Grits 48
Marinated Lamb Chops 50
Crab Cakes 52
Salmon with Cucumber Salsa 54
Grilled Marinated Chicken Breasts 55
Yankee Pot Roast 56
Sautéed Garden Tomato Pasta 58

Table of Contents
continued

Savory Sides 59
POTATO LATKES 61
FRIED GREEN TOMATOES 62
LEMON SESAME COLLARDS 64
AUNT BETTY'S YEAST ROLLS 66
TOMATO BREAD PUDDING 68
ROASTED ASPARAGUS 69
REAL MASHED POTATOES 70
CINNAMON APPLE FRITTERS 71
NOODLE KUGEL 72
ORANGE ORANGE CARROTS 74

Sauces, Relishes and Pickles. 75
APRICOT BBQ SAUCE 77
HONEY MUSTARD DIPPING SAUCE 78
RED BELL PEPPER SAUCE 79
BLENDER HOLLANDAISE 80
GARLIC PEPPER JELLY 82
BLACK BEAN RELISH 83
GINGER PLUM RELISH 84
SUMMER RIPE TOMATO BASIL SALSA 85
BREAD AND BUTTER PICKLES 86
FIRE & ICE RELISH 88

Desserts 89
AUNT TILLIE'S HONEY BALLS 91
BROWN SUGAR POUND CAKE 92

HUDSON VALLEY APPLE PIE 94
BOB'S CHOCOLATE CAKE
   WITH CHOCOLATE SOUR CREAM FROSTING . 96
JAKE ROTHSCHILD'S STRAWBERRY
   BUTTERMILK ICE CREAM 98
NELLIE'S FAVORITE CAKE 99
PEACH RASPBERRY COBBLER 100
OLD-FASHIONED BANANA PUDDING 101
LEMON ICE BOX PIE 102
STRAWBERRIES AND CREAM CHEESECAKE . . . 104
RED VELVET CAKE
   WITH CREAM CHEESE FROSTING 106
WHITE CHOCOLATE BREAD PUDDING
   WITH WHITE CHOCOLATE SAUCE 108
BLUEBERRY CRUMBLE PIE 110

Brunch 111
CATSKILLS SCRAMBLE 113
CHICKEN BISCUIT BENEDICT 114
ALMOST OVER THE TOP BISCUITS 115
RONNIE'S QUICHE 116
COUNTRY GRITS 117
GRIDDLED BUTTERMILK PANCAKES 118
MAPLE PECAN BANANA FRENCH TOAST 120
SOUR CREAM COFFEE CAKE 121

Index 123

Foreword

In 1980 when Glenn Powell first walked into Rich's Cooking School, where I was the director, it was hard to know who was going to teach whom. Already a skilled baker, having trained in the Catskill Mountains as he was growing up, Glenn immediately questioned the merits of learning the classic techniques and theory at the very core of my curriculum. He was openly suspicious of my Southern cooking and the endless testing of different flours in baking loaves of bread and biscuits, and he certainly did not think much of the many hours we spent boning chickens. The unwilling student did however learn. And during the process so did I, while continually witnessing the skillful talents that would bring the Chef and Baker great success.

As he moved through the ranks in the cooking profession, Glenn and I stayed in touch. The Baker often brought tasty treats to the Cooking School. The Menu-Developer and Chef often shared innovative creations at delicious dinners and, somewhere along the way, came his confession that the confidence gained by learning classic cuisine allowed him the freedom to create the numerous delicious dishes that were making him famous.

Now, as Chef-Owner of Agnes & Muriel's restaurant in Atlanta, Glenn showcases his clever twists on fun Americana cuisine—like Mom made, only better. For years, I have anticipated a compilation of the recipes that he has so often prepared for me, such as Lemon Sesame Collards, Corn "Fritters" and of course, his scrumptious biscuits. With the recipes in this book, we can all enjoy Glenn's unique and creative take on the homemade simplicity of comfort food.

As they said at the Cordon Bleu when I was training, "Well done!" My highest compliments to Glenn!

Nathalie Dupree
Nathalie Dupree

Introduction

*W*hat kind of place is Agnes & Muriel's? Well, our customers say "retro" for the funky furniture in the foyer of our 1930s bungalow. And "kitschy" for the pink-and-turquoise color scheme, pasta poodle artwork, old rumba albums and Barbie boxes pinned to the wall. And "homey" for the nurturing portions of comfort food we serve.

For me, it's all of this and more. But mostly, it is the tasty food that we didn't always get at home but wished we had. It all began when, after nearly two decades of slaving over someone else's stove, I decided to take the plunge and open my very own restaurant. With then-coworker Beth Baskin, I put years of experience and ideas into motion, found the right little space and the rest is history.

In November 1995, we opened the doors at Agnes & Muriel's—named for our moms Agnes Baskin and Muriel Powell—to serve good old favorites seven days a week. The concept was an elementary one—literally. A place with a laid-back, fun atmosphere and classic Americana eats on the menu. I'd had enough of the stylized cuisine of the 1970s and '80s served on big white plates that left customers and their wallets empty. Agnes & Muriel's was inspired by *Leave It to Beaver* visions of cozy kitchens: Mom in a campy apron, Betty Crocker and a jar of homemade cookies on the counter, the aroma of a meatloaf with 20 minutes left on the timer.

In this little book of Agnes & Muriel's recipes, I have included many of my favorites. While not approved by Mrs. Cleaver, they are tried and true, and offer the essence of home cooking with a pinch of my own flair thrown in for good measure.

Glenn Powell

Acknowledgments

When I was 13 years old, my older brother Brian turned the key and unlocked the world of cooking for me. One evening my parents and I arrived home and, to our surprise, Brian was in the kitchen baking a batch of Aunt Tillie's Honey Balls. I remember walking into the kitchen amazed that my rather academic brother was cooking—let alone baking—something that tasted just as good as when Mom made it. I believed then and there, without a doubt, that if my brother could cook, then so could I.

Throughout my life, so many people have influenced me in this way, opening doors and de-mystifying the art of creating good food. These individuals and many more have instructed me in tricks of the trade and given me confidence to pursue and succeed.

Thanks especially to my family, for without my roots and inspiration from Muriel to be the best cook I could be, I might not have made it this far. To Nathalie Dupree, for teaching me not to be afraid of food and to try, try again. To Elise Griffin, for classical cooking instruction and a forum in which to be creative. To Beth Baskin, whose talents allowed me to follow my own, for which I am so grateful. And to David Sneed, for a great business partnership and the wonderful balance he lends to our business. Thanks, too, to my staff for contributing to the delicious flavor at Agnes & Muriel's. Special thanks to the folks at Longstreet Press and Marge McDonald for the opportunity to publish this book, and to Elizabeth McDonald for pushing me to meet deadlines, editing my work and sharing my vision for this project.

The **Agnes & Muriel's** *Cafe*

COOKBOOK

*H*ere are the basics for cooking, Agnes & Muriel's style.

This chapter is a collection of notes on ingredients, techniques, recipes, hints and useful information. Hopefully, it will nourish the successful preparation of any recipe in this book or help to inspire variations on these recipes, or your own.

The secret to good cooking and entertaining is to enjoy the process. Have fun and be creative when experimenting with a new recipe or preparing one tried-and-true. The knowledge herein comes from my 20 years of experience, and I guarantee there are a couple of things Mom forgot to tell you.

Caramelized Onions

MAKES 2 ½ CUPS

THIS EASY WAY TO CARAMELIZE ONIONS YIELDS A RICH, FLAVORFUL RESULT.
USE THEM IN QUICHES, SALADS, RELISHES, OMELETS, GRATINS, STEWS AND SOUPS.

2   **large yellow onions, peeled and thinly sliced**
3   **tablespoons vegetable oil**

1. Place onions and vegetable oil in a large skillet.
2. Sauté over very low heat about 30 minutes, stirring often. Onions will begin to sweat and steam.
3. Onions will turn brown and caramelize. Continue to stir, cooking 10 additional minutes.
4. When all onions have reached a golden brown color, remove from heat and use as needed.

Cinnamon Sugar

CINNAMON SUGAR HAS MANY USES AND CAN BE MADE AND STORED. WE SPRINKLE THIS MIXTURE ON TOP OF THE NOODLE KUGEL (PAGE 72) AND WE ROLL EACH CINNAMON APPLE FRITTER (PAGE 71) TO COAT WELL BEFORE SERVING WITH THE GRILLED PORK CHOPS ON PAGE 46. IT'S ALSO GREAT ON FRENCH TOAST.

2   **tablespoons sugar**
1   **teaspoon cinnamon**

1. Mix together in a small bowl.
2. Store any unused portion at room temperature in a zip-top bag or tight-lidded jar.

Egg Wash

MAKES 1 CUP

TO ACHIEVE AN EVEN GOLDEN CRISPY COATING ON FRIED FOOD, DIP FOOD IN THIS WASH BEFORE DREDGING IN BREADING OR FLOUR FOR FRYING. MIX AS NEEDED AND DO NOT STORE ANY LEFTOVER EGG WASH.

2   **eggs, beaten**
⅓   **cup milk**

1. In a small mixing bowl, whisk ingredients together until light golden and fluffy.
2. Dip food thoroughly in egg wash before dredging in dry ingredients and frying in oil or butter.

Piecrust

MAKES TWO 9-INCH PIECRUSTS

2   **cups all-purpose flour**
1   **teaspoon salt**
3   **tablespoons sugar**
⅓   **cup shortening**
⅓   **cup butter, softened**
6   **tablespoons cold water**

1. In a large mixing bowl, stir together flour, salt and sugar.
2. With a knife in each hand, cut shortening and softened butter into flour mixture until well blended. Mixture will be crumbly.
3. Add water 1 tablespoon at a time until dough can be gathered in a ball.

4

4. Divide dough into 2 halves. Place 1 half on a lightly floured board or pastry cloth and, with a floured rolling pin, roll dough evenly to $\frac{1}{8}$-inch thickness and about 3 inches larger than pie plate. If dough should split apart while rolling, simply pinch back together using fingers.

5. Gently fold crust in half and quickly place it into pie plate. Unfold and pat lightly into pie plate. Do not stretch dough to fit pie plate.

6. Using a sharp knife, cut crust around rim, allowing a 1-inch overhang.

7. Crimp edges of crust using thumb and forefinger to pinch dough into decorative design. Or, using a fork dipped in ice water, press tines of fork along edge to seal a 2-crust pie or give a decorative edge to a 1-crust pie.

8. If making a 2-crust pie, fill bottom crust with desired filling and top with second rolled-out crust. Press rim of two crusts together as in Step 7 and bake according to recipe.

9. If making a 1-crust pie, fill and bake according to recipe.

Muriel says:

Unused pie crust may be wrapped tightly in plastic wrap and placed in a zip-top bag in the freezer for up to 1 month or until ready to use. Allow crust to come to room temperature before rolling it and proceeding with pie recipe.

Roasted Nuts

THESE CRISPY TOASTED NUTS ADD PERFECT CRUNCH TO BOTH SWEET AND SAVORY DISHES, INCLUDING PANCAKES, PIES, CAKES, SALADS AND PASTAS. THIS TECHNIQUE CAN BE USED WITH ANY NUT FROM PISTACHIOS TO PINE NUTS, HAZELNUTS, WALNUTS, BLANCHED ALMONDS OR PECANS.

1. Preheat oven to 225°F.
2. Spread desired quantity of nuts in a single layer on a baking sheet.
3. Bake 20 minutes or until nuts begin to turn golden brown.
4. Remove from oven and set aside to cool completely before using as needed.

Soy Dijon Marinade
MAKES ⅔ CUP

IT JUST DOESN'T GET ANY EASIER THAN THIS FOR A SAVORY MARINADE. THIS IS THE BASE FOR THE MARINATED LAMB CHOP RECIPE ON PAGE 50. AS WELL, WE ENHANCE THIS BASIC RECIPE WITH HERBS AND SPICES FOR THE GRILLED MARINATED CHICKEN BREASTS ON PAGE 55 THAT WE USE IN SALADS AND SEVERAL OTHER DISHES THROUGHOUT THE BOOK.

¼ **cup Dijon mustard**
½ **cup Kikkoman soy sauce**

1. In a small mixing bowl, whisk ingredients together until smooth.
2. Refrigerate covered until needed.

The Grill:

Many of the recipes included in this book utilize a charcoal grill. It is a perfect tool for flavorful cooking. If you do not have a charcoal grill because of condo or apartment living, the popular indoor smokeless electric grill is a good substitute.

Special pans are now available in most cooking stores for cooking vegetables on the grill. The pan's surface is covered with holes large enough to allow the cooking process but which prevent veggies falling into the grill.

It is helpful to drop several teaspoons of vegetable oil onto an old rag and wipe it over the grill grate to coat well and prevent food from sticking.

Parchment Paper:

This heavy-duty paper can be found with the aluminum foil and plastic wrap in most large grocery stores. It is great for lining cookie sheets and cake pans, or rolling out a pie crust. When one batch of cookies is done, simply remove the whole sheet of parchment to a wire rack to cool and tear a new one for the next batch. Cleaning is minimized.

Butter:

Unless specified, all of the butter used in this book is unsalted. In days past, salt was added to butter to preserve it. It's much easier to add salt when needed rather than have a dish taste too salty.

Condiments and such:

In some recipes, I call for Thai Fish Sauce or Duck Sauce. These store-bought sauces are excellent for mixing into a marinade or salad dressing and are available in the Oriental section of most large grocery stores.

Eggs:

When I was growing up, we always kept hens and sold their eggs. I remember vividly going with Muriel to gather the eggs, clean and candle them, and rush them off to refrigerated storage. There is nothing like the taste of a fresh egg gently scrambled in fresh butter.

Fresh is truly the only rule for eggs. If an egg is broken or cracked, do not use it. If uncertain of the freshness of an egg, gently place the whole egg in a bowl of cold water; if it sinks, it is good. (Then, discard water and use egg as desired.)

Flour:

All the flour used in my recipes is bleached all-purpose flour except where noted. When sifting is necessary, this step is included in the recipe.

I have found from years of experience that particular flours are crucial to baking well and cooking in general. The type of flour used in a recipe can ruin it or make it a complete success. Cake flour and White Lily plain flour are both great for baking, and in most recipes, all-purpose can be used with success. However, if a recipe calls for a specific brand or kind of flour, always use that flour. The recipe just won't be the same without it.

Herbs and Spices:

The addition of herbs and/or spices to a dish makes it come alive. We use granulated onion and granulated garlic powder quite often. Where needed in recipes, we specify fresh or dried herbs and even in the case of dried herbs, the fresher the better. If the basil in your pantry has been there since you moved in 5 years ago, it's best to replace it with a new batch.

Oils:

For frying or sautéing, vegetable or canola oil is specified in these recipes. When I cook with olive oil, I prefer to use pure olive oil. When I really want to highlight the flavor of the olive oil, I use extra-virgin olive oil.

Salt:

Regular, not iodized, salt may be used without exception in the recipes included and should definitely be used in all baking recipes. If desired, ground sea salt can be substituted equally, or Kosher salt (using about twice the quantity specified) may be used in savory recipes for additional flavor.

Seafood:

Freshness is a necessity for any type of seafood whether it is fish or shellfish. Fresh fish should not smell fishy after being rinsed. It should have clear, firm flesh, not grainy or gray looking.

Sugar:

Use regular granulated sugar in these recipes unless fine sugar is specified. Super-fine sugar is easier to dissolve and may be required when not heating or mixing with a cold liquid. Where brown sugar is called for, it is completely the cook's preference whether dark or light is used. Dark sugar has a slightly stronger molasses flavor than light brown sugar. Of course, if a certain sugar is called for in a recipe, to guarantee success, use that sugar.

Vinegar:

We use lots of vinegar in cooking and in these recipes. I have specified particular vinegars in recipes. Raspberry, balsamic, seasoned rice wine and cider vinegars are available with the white vinegar in most large grocery stores. Seasoned rice wine vinegar is very flavorful due to the addition of sugar and salt. It is delicious when preparing Oriental foods or in vinaigrette for salads or fresh crispy vegetables.

Chopping fresh ginger

This method for chopping ginger is easy and efficient. Especially when using in a marinade, it is not necessary to peel the ginger, which can be a difficult and slippery task.

1. Using the whole gingerroot, or desired portion, slice against the grain into coin-thick disks.
2. Finely chop the disks and use ginger as needed.

Melting chocolate

The trick to successful chocolate melting is absolutely no moisture. Keep all utensils and bowls completely dry.

1. Preheat oven to 200°F.
2. Break or cut chocolate into very small $\frac{1}{2}$-inch pieces.
3. Place the chocolate pieces in a shallow baking pan and place in oven.
4. Check chocolate every 5 minutes and stir to mix well.
5. When chocolate is completely melted, use as needed.

Starters

In Muriel's days of entertaining, appetizers often consisted of deli meats and American cheese rolled into little pinwheels, olives on toothpicks or Pigs-in-a-Blanket. Those times have certainly changed and cooks have become more adventurous with appetizers, especially in restaurants. These days, it is quite popular and great fun when dining out with friends to order several appetizers for the table to share.

Why not try this at home? We encourage the home cook to experiment with a variety of interesting appetizers to successfully open an evening of entertaining, whet the appetite and allow guests to sample your culinary creativity. Salads and pasta dishes served in small portions make engaging appetizers. Or make the meal extra special by offering homemade soup as an elegant first course. Whether presenting starters as a passed or seated course, use your imagination to make a tasty first impression and set the stage for a great meal to follow.

Corn "Fritters"

THOUGH NOT ACTUALLY THE DEEP-FRIED FRITTER COMMONLY THOUGHT OF,
WE CALL THESE LITTLE PANCAKES "FRITTERS" BECAUSE THEY ARE SO FUN AND SO VERY SOUTHERN.

1 cup yellow cornmeal	½ cup milk
¼ cup flour	½ cup sour cream
½ teaspoon baking soda	1 ½ cups canned cream-style corn
½ teaspoon salt	nonstick cooking spray
1 egg	

1. In a medium mixing bowl, sift together the cornmeal, flour, baking soda and salt. Set aside.

2. In a large mixing bowl, whisk egg, milk and sour cream to mix well. Gently stir in canned cream-style corn.

3. Add flour mixture to egg mixture and stir until just blended. Do not overmix, as the pancakes will not cook up light and fluffy.

4. Heat a large skillet or griddle to medium heat. Spray the surface with nonstick cooking spray.

5. Ladle ¼ cup of batter per fritter into the hot skillet or griddle. Cook fritters about 5 minutes to a side. When small bubbles appear on the surface of the fritter, flip and cook the other side until lightly golden.

6. Remove fritters to an ovenproof plate. Place the plate in a warm 250°F oven until all of the fritters are cooked.

To serve:

Serve Corn "Fritters" with Honey Mustard Dipping Sauce (page 78).

Muriel says:

Corn Fritters also make a tasty light lunch when served with sliced homegrown summer tomatoes, or with our Fried Green Tomatoes on page 62 and a tall glass of cold iced tea.

Fried Asparagus

SERVES 4

A DELICIOUS WAY TO PRESENT ASPARAGUS AS AN APPETIZER.

2   eggs, beaten
½   cup milk
1 ½ cups Bisquick
2   teaspoons granulated garlic
1   teaspoon black pepper
1   teaspoon dried basil
1   pound fresh asparagus
        vegetable oil for frying
        Buttermilk Ranch Dressing (page 40)

1. In a small bowl, whisk together eggs and milk. Set aside.

2. In another small bowl, combine Bisquick with garlic, pepper and basil. Set aside.

3. Rinse asparagus well.

4. Trim and discard 2 inches, or more if necessary, of woody stalk from the ends of the asparagus.

5. Add ½ inch of vegetable oil to a medium skillet and heat over medium-high heat.

6. Dip each asparagus spear into egg mixture and then into Bisquick mixture.

7. Place several coated asparagus spears in hot oil and fry until golden, turning often, about 7 minutes.

8. Remove to paper towel to drain.

9. Repeat until all spears are cooked.

To serve:

Plate asparagus spears with a small dish of Buttermilk Ranch Dressing for dipping and serve immediately.

Salmon Croquettes

GROWING UP, EVERYONE'S MOM HAD A DIFFERENT RECIPE FOR SALMON CROQUETTES. MURIEL MADE HERS SWEET WITH CARROTS AND CRUNCHY WITH A HANDFUL OF CORN FLAKES CEREAL.

2	15-ounce cans red salmon
2	teaspoons salt
1	teaspoon black pepper
1	cup chopped caramelized onions (page 3)
½	cup finely shredded carrots
1	cup crushed Corn Flakes cereal or saltine crackers
4	eggs, lightly beaten
¼	cup vegetable oil, for frying

1. Drain and discard liquid from salmon.
2. Remove and discard any skin and bones from salmon.
3. Place salmon in a large bowl and flake gently.
4. Add the salt, pepper, caramelized onions, carrots, crackers or cereal and the eggs. Mix gently but thoroughly.
5. Form into croquettes by scooping a small amount of the salmon mixture into hands. Roll the mixture between palms to form a 2-inch ball.
6. Heat the oil in a large skillet over medium heat.
7. Cook the croquettes until golden, rolling several times to cook all sides.
8. Drain on paper towel.

To serve:

Serve 2 or 3 Salmon Croquettes per person.

Agnes says:

Formed into slightly larger portions, these Croquettes make a fun main course.

Stuffed Portobello Mushrooms

STEAMED AND THEN GRILLED, THESE MUSHROOMS ARE TENDER AND FLAVORFUL.
A GREAT APPETIZER TO SHARE.

2	large portobello mushrooms
¼	cup Soy Dijon Marinade (page 6)
1	tablespoon chopped fresh garlic
1	cup Summer Ripe Tomato Basil Salsa (page 85)
¼	cup crumbled goat's cheese
2	teaspoons chopped fresh parsley leaves

1. Preheat oven to 350°F.
2. Trim and discard woody ends of mushroom stems.
3. Rinse and drain mushrooms well.
4. Place mushrooms upside down in a pie pan and cover with 1 inch of water.
5. Wrap the pie pan with foil and seal it well.
6. Bake for 20 minutes or until mushrooms are tender.
7. Remove mushrooms from pie pan and set aside to dry.
8. In a small mixing bowl, stir together marinade and chopped garlic. Set aside.
9. Prepare hot coals for grilling.
10. Dip the mushrooms into the garlic marinade.
11. Grill on all sides until lightly charred, about 5 minutes.
12. Remove to plates.

Agnes says:

Stuffed Portobello Mushrooms are also tasty with fries on the side and a tossed green salad.

To serve:

Spoon ½ cup of Summer Ripe Tomato Basil Salsa over each mushroom. Sprinkle goat's cheese and parsley over each mushroom.

Baked Potato Soup

SERVES 10

I HAVE BEEN MAKING THIS SOUP FOR YEARS. IT IS EASY TO PUT TOGETHER
AND WONDERFUL TO SERVE TO A LARGE CROWD OF HUNGRY FOLKS.

6	medium Russet potatoes, baked, cooled, peeled and cubed into ¾-inch pieces
2	tablespoons butter
1	large peeled and diced yellow onion
1 ½	cups diced celery
8	cups half-and-half
1	tablespoon salt
2	teaspoons black pepper
3	tablespoons additional butter
⅓	cup flour
	sour cream
	cooked bacon
	chopped fresh chives
	grated cheddar cheese

To serve:

Ladle hot soup into bowls and top with a dollop of sour cream, crumbled bacon, chopped chives and a sprinkling of grated cheddar cheese.

1. In a heavy 6-quart pot, melt 2 tablespoons butter over medium heat.
2. Add onion and celery and cook 15 minutes, stirring often.
3. Pour in half-and-half, and add salt and black pepper. Continue to heat, stirring often, until boiling.
4. Meanwhile, in a small skillet, melt 3 tablespoons butter and whisk in flour. Cook while whisking 5 minutes over medium heat.
5. Ladle a small amount of warm half-and-half mixture into skillet and whisk to blend with flour mixture.
6. Pour this back into soup and whisk well to dissolve. Soup will begin to thicken.
7. Add cubed potatoes and cook 20 minutes, stirring often.
8. Stir well and season to taste with salt and pepper before serving.

Roasted Elephant Garlic

SERVES 2-4

ON A RESTAURANT RESEARCH TRIP MANY YEARS AGO, I WAS SERVED THIS DELICIOUS DISH IN VERO BEACH, FLORIDA, AND IMMEDIATELY LOVED IT. IT HAS BEEN A STAPLE IN MY REPERTOIRE EVER SINCE. AT AGNES & MURIEL'S WE SERVE ROASTED ELEPHANT GARLIC AS AN APPETIZER ALONGSIDE ROASTED SUN-DRIED TOMATOES, FRESH GOAT'S CHEESE AND WARM FRENCH BREAD.

1	**whole head elephant garlic**
1	**tablespoon pure olive oil**
	pinch of salt
	freshly ground black pepper to taste
	French bread
1	**3.5-ounce block fresh goat's cheese**
1	**4-ounce jar sun-dried tomatoes, in olive oil**

1. Preheat oven to 300°F.
2. Peel the papery skins off garlic cloves and discard.
3. In a small bowl, toss whole garlic cloves with olive oil, salt and pepper to coat well.
4. Place garlic on a large square of aluminum foil and wrap ingredients tightly to seal foil as in an airtight pouch.
5. Bake garlic until tender, about 45 minutes. When done, the garlic should be easily pierced with a dull knife and spreadable.

To serve:

Place warm Roasted Elephant Garlic on a plate and top with crumbled goat's cheese. Place a small amount of roasted sun-dried tomatoes next to garlic and surround with pieces of warm French bread.

Cucumber Dill Vichyssoise

SERVES 12

THIS IS AN EASY VERSION OF A CLASSIC SOUP. IT NEVER FAILS TO BECOME A FAVORITE OF THOSE WHO TRY IT.
REMEMBER TO PLAN FOR TIME IN THE FRIDGE TO CHILL THE SOUP BEFORE SERVING.

10	medium peeled and diced red potatoes
2	large peeled, seeded and diced cucumbers
1	large peeled and diced yellow onion
5	cups chicken stock
1	teaspoon white pepper
1	teaspoon salt
¼	cup sour cream
2	cups heavy cream
1	tablespoon freshly squeezed lemon juice
¼	cup chopped fresh dill
	fresh dill for garnish

To serve:

Serve ice-cold Cucumber Dill
Vichyssoise in chilled bowls with
a sprig of dill for garnish.

1. In a heavy 6-quart pot, place potatoes, cucumbers, onions, chicken stock and white pepper, and bring to a boil over medium-high heat.

2. Cook until vegetables are tender, about 20 minutes.

3. Remove from heat and add remaining ingredients to potato mixture.

4. Working in batches, blend small amounts of potato mixture with blender or food processor until all the soup is completely smooth.

5. Transfer blended soup to a large bowl. Cover and refrigerate 8 hours or overnight until well chilled.

6. Stir well and adjust seasoning to taste before serving.

Summer Gazpacho

THIS SIMPLE CHILLED SOUP IS BURSTING WITH SUMMER FLAVORS.

4	cups (or 2 11-ounce cans) whole plum tomatoes with juice, diced into ½-inch pieces
1	46-ounce can tomato juice
3	cups unpeeled and diced pickling cucumbers
2	cups diced green bell peppers
1 ½	cups sliced green onions
1	teaspoon dried tarragon
2	teaspoons garlic salt
1	teaspoon Tabasco
⅓	cup red wine vinegar
⅓	cup granulated sugar
1	teaspoon white pepper
1	teaspoon celery salt
	salt and pepper to taste
1	pint sour cream
	croutons

1. *P*our diced canned tomatoes with juice into a large mixing bowl.

2. Add next 12 ingredients and stir well.

3. Refrigerate for at least 4 hours and then stir well before serving.

To serve:

Ladle portions of soup into chilled bowls. Top with a dollop of sour cream and sprinkle with croutons.

Muriel says:

Summer Gazpacho will stay fresh for 2 days if well chilled.

Smoked Salmon Chowder

SERVES 12

RICH AND CREAMY AND STEEPED WITH FLAVOR, THIS SOUP IS GREAT JUST ABOUT ANY TIME—
BUT ESPECIALLY WHEN THERE IS A CHILL IN THE AIR.

2	tablespoons butter
1	cup peeled and diced yellow onion
1	cup diced celery
4	tablespoons additional butter
½	cup flour
3	cups half-and-half
3	cups canned corn
1 ½	cups cream style canned corn
1 ½	teaspoons black pepper
1 ½	teaspoons sugar
2	cups milk
1	pound prepared smoked salmon, cut into 1-inch pieces
¼	cup chopped fresh dill
	fresh dill for garnish

1. In a large skillet, melt 2 tablespoons butter and add onion and celery. Sauté over medium heat until tender, about 15 minutes.

2. Meanwhile, in a 6-quart stockpot, melt butter over medium heat and whisk in flour. While whisking, cook 5 minutes.

3. Add onion mixture and all remaining ingredients except dill to stockpot. Stir well.

4. Bring chowder to a boil over medium heat, stirring often.

5. When chowder reaches a boil, add dill and adjust seasonings to taste before serving.

To *serve:*

Ladle chowder into soup bowls and garnish with fresh dill. Serve immediately.

Crab Bisque

THIS SOUP IS PARTICULARLY IMPRESSIVE AS A FIRST COURSE FOR SPECIAL OCCASIONS OR HOLIDAY DINNERS.

12	ounces fresh lump crabmeat
2	sticks butter
3	cups diced yellow onion
2	cups shredded and diced carrots
1	cup chopped fresh green onion
1	tablespoon peeled, finely chopped fresh garlic
2	tablespoons tomato paste
¾	cup flour
1	cup Sherry
2 ½	cups fish stock
5	cups half-and-half
¼	cup freshly squeezed lemon juice
1	teaspoon salt
1	teaspoon celery salt
1	teaspoon white pepper
1 ½	teaspoons chopped fresh parsley
	fresh parsley for garnish

To serve:

Ladle hot soup into soup bowls and garnish with a sprig of fresh parsley. Serve immediately.

Agnes says:

Homemade fish stock can sometimes be found in specialty gourmet markets. It may also be purchased in most large grocery stores with the bouillon and soup mixes. Remember, if using it in bouillon form, it's necessary to reconstitute with water before proceeding with recipe.

1. Pick through crabmeat and discard any shells. Set aside.
2. In a heavy 6-quart pot, melt butter over medium heat.
3. Add onions, carrots, green onion, garlic and tomato paste. Sauté over medium heat until vegetables are tender, about 15 minutes.
4. Whisk flour into vegetables and cook 5 minutes.
5. Add all remaining ingredients and simmer for 10 minutes, stirring often.
6. Stir well and adjust seasoning to taste before serving.

Salads

*I*n the old days at home, salad was a wedge of Iceberg lettuce and a cruet of dressing set directly on the table. Imagine my surprise when I moved to the South and found that the word *salad* meant more than just a wedge of lettuce. Its meaning also included a cold congealed salad with marshmallows and cherries or a side serving of creamy potato salad.

Salads have come a long way since I sat at the old Formica-and-chrome dinette set in Muriel's kitchen. With an abundance of fresh produce available today, the home cook can easily create enjoyable, healthy salads any time of year. Using the freshest ingredients and premium olive oils, vinegars, herbs, or perhaps one of the dressing recipes included in this chapter, a salad becomes a satisfying, delicious meal or a gratifying side dish.

We offer our own versions of modern main course and side-salads every day. And, as a throwback to the early days, you can still order a wedge of Iceberg lettuce at Agnes & Muriel's. We'll even serve that salad with a cruet full of Green Goddess dressing set directly on the table, if you like.

Michelle's Cabbage Slaw

SERVES 10

A RECIPE FROM A GOOD FRIEND, THIS IS NOT TYPICAL SLAW WITH MAYONNAISE IN THE DRESSING; IT IS MORE OF A MARINATED CABBAGE SALAD. GREAT PICNIC FOOD.

For slaw:

1	head green cabbage, shredded
1	large cucumber, unpeeled and sliced thin
2	large chopped green bell peppers
1	small bunch fresh parsley, chopped (about 1 ½ cups)
2	cups diced celery
1	cup chopped green onions

For dressing:

4	cloves peeled fresh garlic
1	cup white vinegar
¾	cup sugar
1	teaspoon kosher salt
½	teaspoon black pepper
1	cup vegetable oil

For slaw:

1. In a large mixing bowl combine shredded cabbage, cucumber, green bell pepper, parsley, celery and green onion. Toss well to mix vegetables and set aside.

For dressing:

1. Place garlic in the bowl of a food processor fitted with steel blade. Pulse to chop garlic finely.
2. Add remaining dressing ingredients except oil and pulse several additional times to mix.
3. Add oil in a slow stream while processor is running. Blend until oil is well combined.
4. Pour dressing over vegetable mixture.
5. Cover and refrigerate 4 hours or overnight until ready to serve.

To serve:

Stir Slaw well and serve chilled.

Muriel says:

For the most flavorful slaw, when shredding cabbage, make sure to remove the tough outer green leaves. Shred the inside green leaves and the core of the cabbage, which is pale green or white.

Carmen Miranda Chicken Salad

SERVES 4

CARMEN MIRANDA WAS KNOWN FOR HER ELABORATE HEADDRESSES MADE OF FRUIT. SOMETIMES AT AGNES & MURIEL'S, WHEN THINGS GET A LITTLE NUTTY, WE FEEL LIKE WEARING THIS SALAD ON OUR HEADS! CARAMBA!

1	fresh pineapple
1	fresh mango
1 ½	cups shredded carrots
2	cups bean sprouts
¼	cup chopped fresh cilantro leaves
1 ½	cups Lime Dressing (below)
6	cups assorted salad greens, washed, drained and chopped
½	cup Peanut Dressing (below)
4	Grilled Marinated Chicken Breasts, cut into ½-inch dice (page 55)
1	cup sweetened banana chips
½	cup roasted salted cashew halves
1	pound red seedless grapes, divided into 4 servings

1. Cut the whole pineapple lengthwise into quarters, leaving the fronds (leaves) attached.
2. Cut the core from the middle of each pineapple piece.
3. To separate the pineapple from the rind, slide a sharp knife between the fleshy part of the fruit and the rind, still leaving the fronds attached. Set the rinds aside.
4. Dice the pineapple fruit into ¼-inch pieces and place it in a large mixing bowl.
5. Peel skin from mango and remove pit. Dice fruit into ¼-inch pieces. Add to pineapple.
6. Add shredded carrots to pineapple mixture.
7. Add bean sprouts, cilantro and salad greens to pineapple mixture.
8. Drizzle Lime Dressing over fruit and greens. Toss well to coat.

Agnes says:

Fresh mango may be available already peeled and prepared in the produce section of large grocery stores.

To serve:

1. Place one piece of pineapple rind (with fronds) into each of four large salad bowls (or plates), rind side down. Let the fronds hang over the edge of each bowl or plate.
2. Mound the fruit salad mixture on top of pineapple shells.
3. Drizzle Peanut Dressing over the salad.
4. Top with the diced chicken.
5. Sprinkle each salad with banana chips and cashews.
6. Garnish with a cluster of red grapes.

Lime Dressing
MAKES 3 CUPS

1 ½	**cups freshly squeezed lime juice**
1	**cup light brown sugar**
½	**cup Thai Fish Sauce**

1. In a medium mixing bowl, whisk all ingredients together. Make sure to dissolve any little lumps of brown sugar.
2. Chill one hour to allow flavors to marry.
3. Shake or stir well before adding to salad.

Muriel says:
For a tasty grilling sauce, baste both sides of chicken or shrimp liberally with this dressing while cooking. Be sure to heat any remaining sauce to boiling in a small saucepan over medium heat for five minutes before serving it alongside the chicken or shrimp.

Peanut Dressing
MAKES 3 ¼ CUPS

2	**cups bottled Duck Sauce**
½	**cup mayonnaise**
½	**cup creamy peanut butter**
¼	**cup milk**

1. In a medium mixing bowl, whisk all ingredients together until smooth.
2. Chill dressing one hour before serving.

Grilled Garlic Broccoli Salad

AN ALTERNATIVE TO STEAMED VEGETABLES, THIS RECIPE IS GREAT WHEN YOU KNOW YOU WILL BE HEATING UP THE BBQ.

1	**large head of fresh broccoli**
1	**tablespoon salt**
	nonstick cooking spray
½	**cup extra-virgin olive oil**
1	**tablespoon peeled and chopped fresh garlic**
	additional salt and black pepper to taste

To blanch broccoli:

1. Bring a large pot of water to a boil.
2. While waiting for water to boil, trim and discard the woody stem ends from the broccoli. Cut the broccoli into medium-sized pieces not too small for grilling. Set aside.
3. Add the broccoli and 1 tablespoon of salt to the boiling water and boil for 5 minutes uncovered.
4. While broccoli cooks, fill a 3 or 4-quart bowl with ice water.
5. Remove broccoli to the ice water and allow broccoli to cool completely. This preserves a bright green color.
6. Drain broccoli well.

Broccoli may be prepared to this point and chilled for several hours (or overnight) before proceeding.

Grilling broccoli:

1. Prepare hot coals for grilling.
2. Spray broccoli generously with nonstick cooking spray and place directly on hot grill. Cook broccoli, turning often, until sides begin to char, about 7 minutes on a hot grill. Remove from heat and set aside.

Agnes says:

This salad is great any time of year and will keep for 2 days refrigerated. The broccoli may absorb the oil, so add a few tablespoons and toss well to coat just before serving.

To finish salad:

1. In a small saucepan or skillet, heat olive oil and garlic over medium heat. Cook garlic until tender, about 7 minutes. Do not brown the garlic. Remove from heat and allow to cool.
2. In a large mixing bowl, toss the broccoli with the garlic and olive oil mixture together. Season with additional salt and pepper if desired.
3. Chill salad one hour before serving.

To serve:

Serve cold Broccoli Salad as a side dish.

Peanut Pickled Beets

SERVES 8

THIS RECIPE IS EASY AND DELICIOUS. THE PEANUTS ADD FUN CRUNCH.

4	cups canned sliced beets with liquid
1 ½	cups sugar
1 ½	cups white vinegar
2	tablespoons pickling spice
1	cup roasted salted peanuts, chopped coarsely
½	cup green onions, finely chopped

1. Place beets with liquid, sugar, vinegar and spices in a large saucepan.
2. Bring to a boil over medium heat.
3. Reduce heat to medium-low and simmer for 5 minutes.
4. Remove from heat and allow to cool completely.

Beets may be prepared to this point and refrigerated for up to one week.

To serve:

Strain beets from liquid, sprinkle peanuts and green onion over beets and serve as a side dish.

Watermelon Vidalia Salad

VIDALIA ONIONS ARE MILD, SWEET AND AVAILABLE NATIONWIDE THROUGHOUT THE SUMMER MONTHS. SOME PEOPLE IN THE SOUTH EVEN EAT THEM LIKE APPLES. WE LIKE THEM MIXED WITH A LITTLE SWEET VINEGAR AND COLD WATERMELON.

This salad is true Georgia summertime!

4 **cups watermelon, rind and seeds removed, and cut into 1-inch cubes**
¾ **cup peeled and very thinly sliced Vidalia Onions**
½ **cup high quality raspberry vinegar**
sugar to taste (optional)

1. In a large mixing bowl, gently toss watermelon cubes with sliced onions and raspberry vinegar.
2. Cover salad and refrigerate for at least 2 hours before serving to allow flavors to marry.
3. Taste salad just before serving and add 1 or 2 tablespoons of sugar if necessary.

To serve:

This salad is best served ice cold and eaten within 4 hours of preparing.

Agnes says:

If Vidalia Onions are not available, Texas or Washington State Sweet onions may be substituted.

Grilled Lettuce Caesar Salad with Caesar Dressing

AN EASY AND INNOVATIVE TAKE ON A TRADITIONAL RECIPE, THIS SALAD IS A PERFECT ADDITION TO A FAMILY DINNER PREPARED ON THE BBQ.

1	head of romaine lettuce
	nonstick cooking spray
⅔	cup Caesar Salad Dressing (below)
¼	cup shaved Parmigiano-Reggiano cheese
½	cup croutons

1. Prepare hot coals for grilling.
2. Leaving the head of romaine intact, trim and discard any bruised outer leaves.
3. Wash lettuce well, running water into the head. Drain the lettuce well.
4. Cut romaine lettuce in half lengthwise, leaving the core intact.
5. Spray the lettuce liberally with nonstick cooking spray.
6. Grill lettuce on all sides until leaves begin to char, about 4 minutes to a side on a hot grill.

To serve:

Cut the lettuce into quarters and plate with the cut side up. Drizzle Caesar Salad Dressing evenly over lettuce and top with shaved Parmigiano-Reggiano and croutons.

Caesar Salad Dressing

MAKES 3 ½ CUPS

¼	cup anchovy paste
2	tablespoons Worcestershire sauce
⅔	cup freshly squeezed lemon juice
2	tablespoons chopped fresh garlic
½	cup mayonnaise
1 ½	teaspoons Dijon mustard
2	cups pure olive oil

1. In a large mixing bowl, whisk anchovy paste, Worcestershire sauce, lemon juice and garlic together.
2. Add mayonnaise and Dijon mustard, and stir to blend.
3. While whisking constantly, slowly add olive oil to anchovy mixture. Continue whisking until oil is thoroughly combined.

Balsamic Dressing

THIS IS ONE OF OUR MOST REQUESTED DRESSINGS—AND JUST THINK, IT'S VERY LOW IN FAT!

1 ½ **cups buttermilk**
½ **cup balsamic vinegar**
1 ½ **teaspoons Dijon mustard**
2 **teaspoons chopped fresh garlic**
1 ½ **teaspoons chopped fresh rosemary leaves**
½ **cup diced, unpeeled cucumbers**
½ **cup carrots, shredded**

1. To the bowl of a food processor or blender, add buttermilk, balsamic vinegar, Dijon mustard, chopped garlic and rosemary. Pulse once or twice to just blend. Scrape down sides of bowl.
2. Add cucumbers and carrots to buttermilk mixture.
3. Blend until vegetables are finely chopped but not puréed.
4. Chill dressing one hour before serving.

Agnes says:

This dressing is great served over Bibb lettuce with sliced tomatoes and cucumbers or your favorite salad greens.

Green Goddess Dressing

MAKES 2 CUPS

WE HAVE NOTICED MANY RESTAURANTS UPDATING THE NAME OF THIS OLD-FASHIONED FAVORITE.
WE MODERNIZED THE RECIPE WITH FRESH HERBS AND A LITTLE ANCHOVY PASTE, BUT WE KEPT THE GREAT NAME.

½ teaspoon chopped fresh garlic
1 teaspoon anchovy paste
2 tablespoons chopped fresh parsley
2 tablespoons chopped fresh chives
¼ teaspoon dried tarragon
1 teaspoon garlic salt
2 teaspoons black pepper
1 tablespoon freshly squeezed lemon juice
2 tablespoons white vinegar
¾ cup sour cream
1 cup mayonnaise

1. In the bowl of a food processor fitted with a steel blade, pulse the garlic and anchovy paste to mix well.
2. Add parsley, chives, tarragon, salt, pepper, lemon juice and vinegar, and pulse several more times to combine.
3. Transfer mixture to a large mixing bowl and stir in sour cream and mayonnaise.
4. Cover tightly and chill at least 2 hours or until ready to serve.

To serve:

Stir dressing well before serving over your favorite green salad.

Buttermilk Ranch Dressing

MAKES 3 ½ CUPS

IN THE LATE '80'S, WHEN I WANTED TO ADD RANCH DRESSING TO A MENU I WAS WORKING ON, I COULD NOT LOCATE A RECIPE FOR IT ANYWHERE. I EVEN CALLED THE PUBLIC LIBRARY'S RESEARCH OFFICE AND HAD THEM CHECK FOR ONE. IT SEEMS THAT HIDDEN VALLEY "INVENTED" RANCH DRESSING. BEFORE THAT COMPANY'S TIME, THERE ARE NOT ANY PUBLISHED RECIPES FOR RANCH DRESSING AS WE KNOW IT. THE SECRET INGREDIENTS IN MY RECIPE ARE ONION POWDER AND BUTTERMILK.

2   cups mayonnaise
½   cup sour cream
1   cup buttermilk
1   tablespoon plus 2 teaspoons onion powder
1 ½ teaspoons garlic powder
1 ½ teaspoons black pepper
1 ½ teaspoons dried parsley flakes

1. In a medium mixing bowl, whisk mayonnaise and sour cream together until smooth.
2. Gradually add in the buttermilk and continue to whisk until the mixture is very smooth.
3. Add the remaining ingredients and whisk to blend.
4. Chill one hour and stir well before serving.

Muriel says:

We serve this dressing as a dipping sauce with Fried Asparagus (page 16). It is also very good with raw or roasted vegetables, or a green salad.

Entrées

Agnes & Muriel's is a lot about comfort food. So many restaurants these days present frilly food on fancy plates with swirling sauces for decoration that is almost too pretty to eat. My goal is to serve straightforward, good food in a not-so-glamorous way. Our china may not always match, but we guarantee you won't notice. We serve healthy portions of good old favorites, just like Mom lovingly dished up. And, if it happens to be Wednesday night and Pot Roast is our special, you just might wonder if it really is she back in the kitchen.

Cracked Mustard Seed Chicken

MAKES ABOUT 3 ½ CUPS SAUCE,
SERVES 6

¼ cup whole grain mustard
1 cup Dijon mustard
2 ½ cups heavy whipping cream
2 teaspoons freshly squeezed lemon juice
¼ teaspoon white pepper
¼ teaspoon salt
2 teaspoons peeled and chopped fresh garlic
6 large boneless, skinless chicken breasts

To serve:

Provide small individual dishes with Mustard Sauce alongside grilled chicken breasts. Serve with Lemon Sesame Collards (page 64) and homemade squash casserole.

For sauce:

1. Stir first 7 ingredients together in a large saucepan and place over medium-low heat.
2. When mixture begins to boil, reduce heat to low and, stirring often, cook for 30 minutes. Sauce will reduce by about ⅓. Sauce can be made ahead and after cooling should be stored covered in the refrigerator.

For chicken:

1. Rinse chicken breasts well and drain on paper towel.
2. Place chicken breasts in a shallow baking pan and pour 1 cup of Mustard Sauce over chicken. Turn to coat well. Save remaining sauce for basting and serving.
3. Prepare hot coals for grilling.
4. Remove chicken from Mustard Sauce and discard any sauce left in the pan.
5. Cook chicken breasts to desired doneness, turning once and basting both sides with a little mustard sauce.
6. Remove from grill and plate chicken.

BBQ Baby Back Ribs and Rib Rub

SERVES 4-6

SINCE COOKING RIBS SLOWLY OVER A HUGE OPEN PIT BBQ IS VIRTUALLY IMPOSSIBLE IN A RESTAURANT KITCHEN,
I DEVISED THIS METHOD OF STEAMING THE RIBS BEFORE FINISHING THEM OVER HOT CHARCOAL.
THE RESULT IS A TENDER AND JUICY RACK OF RIBS. OUTSTANDING FLAVOR!

3	**slabs baby back ribs**
¾	**cup Rib Rub (below)**
2	**cups water**
3	**tablespoons Liquid Smoke flavoring**
	prepared BBQ sauce as needed
	for grilling and dipping

Agnes says:

You may steam the ribs up to 3 days before grilling. Allow them to come to room temperature before grilling.

1. Preheat oven to 250°F.
2. Rub the ribs evenly with the Rib Rub.
3. Place a single layer of ribs into a large roasting pan with the curved side up.
4. Add water and liquid smoke to the pan.
5. Wrap the roasting pan tightly with plastic wrap.
6. Wrap the roasting pan again with aluminum foil.
7. Bake for 2 ½ hours or until ribs are very tender.
8. To finish ribs on the BBQ, prepare hot coals for grilling.
9. Grill until browned, basting both sides of ribs liberally with BBQ sauce. About 7 minutes to a side.

To serve:

Cut each slab into individual ribs and serve with plenty of extra BBQ sauce for dipping.

Rib Rub

MAKES 2 ½ CUPS

½	cup salt
¼	cup ground black pepper
¼	cup granulated garlic
2	tablespoons ground cumin
½	cup brown sugar
1 ½	teaspoons cayenne pepper
½	cup sugar
¼	cup chili powder

Muriel says:

This rub is tasty on any hearty meat that will be grilled, especially pork. Also, try it rubbed on a turkey or chicken breast before grilling or smoking. Rib Rub will keep for several weeks in an airtight container or zip-top bag at room temperature.

1. In a large mixing bowl, combine all ingredients and stir well to remove any lumps of brown sugar.
2. Rinse ribs or meat and pat dry.
3. Rub a generous amount of Rib Rub all over the outside of meat and proceed with grilling.

Grilled Pork Chops with Cinnamon Apple Fritters

SERVES 6

THIS IS MY TAKE ON "PORK CHOPS AND APPLESAUCE." THESE CHOPS NEED TIME TO MARINATE, SO IT IS BEST TO START THIS RECIPE THE DAY BEFORE YOU PLAN TO SERVE IT.

½ **cup Soy Dijon marinade (page 6)**
¼ **cup chopped fresh sage**
6 **¾-inch-thick pork chops**
6 **Cinnamon Apple Fritters (page 71)**

Muriel says:

When marinating, it is a good idea to turn meat several times to insure tenderness and even flavor.

1. In a large 2-inch deep baking dish or pan, stir together marinade and sage. Place pork chops in marinade, turning to coat well. Cover dish and marinate for at least 12 hours or overnight in the refrigerator.

2. Prepare hot coals for grilling.

3. Grill pork chops until desired degree of doneness, about 10 minutes to a side. To assure doneness, it is best to check the internal temperature of the chops with a meat thermometer.

4. Remove the chops from the grill and plate them.

To serve:

Top each Grilled Pork Chop with a Cinnamon Apple Fritter and serve immediately.

Turkey Meatloaf

SERVES 6

A DELICIOUS VERSION OF THE MEATLOAF MURIEL USED TO MAKE. FOR THIS RECIPE, BUY PREMIUM GROUND TURKEY; IT USUALLY HAS MORE BREAST MEAT AND IS LEANER AND MORE FLAVORFUL.

1	medium yellow onion, peeled and very finely chopped	1 $\frac{1}{2}$	teaspoons black pepper
2	eggs	1	cup breadcrumbs
$\frac{1}{3}$	cup catsup	1	cup quick oats
1	tablespoon soy sauce	1	cup hot milk (skim or whole)
1	tablespoon Dijon mustard	2	pounds ground turkey meat
$\frac{1}{2}$	teaspoon salt		parchment paper or nonstick cooking spray

1. *L*ine a large loaf pan with parchment paper or spray liberally with nonstick cooking spray and set aside.
2. Preheat oven to 350°F.
3. Combine onion, eggs, catsup, soy sauce, mustard, salt and pepper in a small mixing bowl. Stir well and set aside.
4. In a large mixing bowl mix breadcrumbs, oats and hot milk. Stir well.
5. Add turkey to breadcrumb mixture and stir to combine thoroughly.
6. Add onion mixture to turkey and stir well. Make sure to incorporate all of onion mixture into turkey mixture.
7. Pat turkey mixture into loaf pan.
8. Bake 1 $\frac{1}{2}$ hours or until center of meatloaf reaches 160°F on a meat thermometer.
9. Remove from oven and allow meatloaf to rest 10 minutes before serving.

To serve:

Serve Turkey Meatloaf hot as a main course—or it is delicious the next day on an open-faced sandwich with a little extra catsup.

Louisiana BBQ Shrimp over Country Grits

SERVES 6-8

LOUISIANA-STYLE BBQ IS SLOW SIMMERED IN BUTTER, OIL AND HERBS. IN CAJUN COUNTRY, THESE SHRIMP WOULD STILL HAVE THEIR SHELLS ON WHEN THEY ARRIVE AT THE TABLE. LEAVE THE TAILS ON AND DEVEIN THE FRESHEST SHRIMP YOU CAN FIND FOR THIS RECIPE. SERVE THEM ON A BED OF OUR CREAMY COUNTRY GRITS (PAGE 117).

2	pounds large shrimp, shelled with tails left on, deveined	2	tablespoons dried rosemary
1	pound butter	1	teaspoon dried basil
2	cups oil	1	teaspoon dried oregano
2	tablespoons chopped fresh garlic	1	teaspoon ground cayenne pepper
		2	tablespoons paprika
1 ½	teaspoons salt	1 ½	teaspoons black pepper
		2	teaspoons freshly squeezed lemon juice
		1	recipe Country Grits (page 117)

1. Peel and devein shrimp.
2. Rinse shrimp well and set them aside to drain.
3. In a large deep skillet or sauté pan, melt butter and oil.
4. Add remaining ingredients except for shrimp and simmer for 30 minutes over very low heat. This infuses butter and oil with herbs and seasonings.
5. Add shrimp and sauté, turning often, about 7 minutes or until shrimp are cooked through.
6. Remove from heat and serve immediately.

To serve:

Spoon a generous helping of grits onto each plate. Divide shrimp between plates and spoon on top of grits. Top with buttery gravy.

Marinated Lamb Chops

CUSTOMERS CONSTANTLY ASK FOR THIS ENTRÉE. PLAN AHEAD FOR AT LEAST
12 HOURS OF MARINATING TIME TO FULLY FLAVOR AND TENDERIZE THE CHOPS.

1	Soy Dijon Marinade (page 6)
¼	cup chopped fresh garlic
¼	cup chopped fresh rosemary leaves
2	tablespoons brown sugar
8	small (about ¾-pound each) lamb chops

1. In a large baking dish or shallow pan, mix together marinade, garlic, rosemary and brown sugar. Stir well.
2. Place chops in marinade and turn several times to coat.
3. Cover tightly and refrigerate at least 12 hours or overnight.
4. Remove chops from refrigerator 1 hour prior to cooking.
5. Prepare hot coals for grilling.
6. Grill lamb chops until desired degree of doneness, about 7 minutes to a side on a hot grill. To assure doneness, it is best to check the internal temperature of the chops with a meat thermometer.
7. Remove chops to plate and serve immediately.

To serve:

Serve Marinated Lamb Chops with Real Mashed Potatoes (page 70) and a side of Roasted Asparagus (page 69).

Crab Cakes

A REAL TREAT, THESE CAKES ARE MADE WITH LUMP CRABMEAT.

1	pound fresh lump crabmeat
2	cups finely ground saltine crackers
1	tablespoon vegetable oil
1	cup peeled and diced yellow onion
½	cup chopped green onion
½	cup mayonnaise
1	egg, beaten
¼	teaspoon ground cayenne pepper
1	teaspoon Tabasco
1 ½	teaspoon Old Bay seasoning
½	teaspoons black pepper
1	tablespoon Worcestershire sauce
1	cup additional saltine crackers, crushed by hand
3	tablespoons additional vegetable oil
	Red Bell Pepper Sauce (page 79)

1. *P*ick through crabmeat and discard any shells. Set aside.
2. Place saltine crackers in bowl of food processor and pulse several times to grind finely. Measure 2 cups and set aside.
3. In a large skillet, heat vegetable oil. Add onion. Sauté over medium heat until onions just wilt. Do not brown.
4. Remove from heat, add green onions, stir well and set aside to cool.
5. In a large mixing bowl, whisk mayonnaise and egg with next 5 ingredients.
6. Add onion mixture to mixing bowl and stir well.

7. Break 1 cup of saltine crackers by hand and add to mixing bowl.

8. Gently stir in crabmeat.

9. Using hands, form 6 patties and roll each in the 2 cups of finely ground saltine crackers to coat.

10. In a large skillet, heat 3 tablespoons vegetable oil and sauté crab cakes over medium heat. Turn and cook until both sides are golden brown.

11. Remove to paper towel to drain.

To serve:

Place 2 crab cakes on each plate and top with a hearty spoonful of Red Bell Pepper Sauce. Serve immediately.

Salmon with Cucumber Salsa

SERVES 6

GREAT GRILLED FARE IN THE HOT SUMMERTIME. I SUGGEST MAKING THE SALSA A FEW HOURS
(OR A DAY) BEFORE COOKING THE FISH, SO IT WILL BE WELL CHILLED.

For salsa:

2	cups unpeeled, diced cucumber
1	cup chopped green onion
⅓	cup seasoned rice wine vinegar
1	teaspoon freshly squeezed lemon juice
½	teaspoon black pepper
¼	cup finely chopped fresh dill

For salmon:

6	fresh salmon steaks, 1-inch thick
	salt
	additional pepper

For salsa:

1. In a large bowl, toss together cucumber, green onion, vinegar, lemon juice, pepper and dill. Cover tightly and chill 2 hours.

For salmon:

1. Rinse salmon steaks well and pat dry.
2. Sprinkle salmon generously on both sides with salt and pepper.
3. Prepare hot coals for grilling.
4. Grill salmon steaks until flesh pales in color and flakes, about 7 minutes to a side.

To serve:

Remove salmon to plates and generously top each steak with a spoonful of salsa. Serve immediately.

Grilled Marinated Chicken Breasts

This basic marinated chicken recipe is delicious on its own as a main course, or use it in the Chicken Biscuit Benedict on page 114 or in the Carmen Miranda Chicken Salad on page 30 for a little variety.

1	Soy Dijon Marinade (page 6)
¼	cup chopped fresh garlic
2	teaspoons dried oregano
2	teaspoons dried parsley
3	tablespoons brown sugar
1	teaspoon black pepper
6	large boneless, skinless chicken breasts

1. Stir together first 6 ingredients in a large bowl.
2. Place chicken breasts in a shallow baking dish or roasting pan.
3. Pour marinade over chicken breasts and turn them once or twice to coat well.
4. Place in refrigerator for at least 6 hours before proceeding to grill chicken.
5. Prepare hot coals for grilling.
6. Place chicken breasts on hot grill. Reserve marinade for basting. Cook 5 minutes.
7. Liberally brush chicken breasts and turn to cook other side 5 minutes or until chicken breast is cooked through.

To serve:

Grilled Marinated Chicken can be served immediately off the grill, or allow the chicken to cool and wrap tightly before refrigerating for future use.

Yankee Pot Roast

I PUT A GOURMET TWIST ON MURIEL'S OLD STAND-BY.

4   **cups beef stock or bouillon**
3   **cups white wine**
½   **cup brandy**
2   **tablespoons vegetable oil**
3   **cups peeled and sliced yellow onions**
2   **tablespoons canned tomato paste**
2   **tablespoons chopped fresh garlic**
3   **cups canned tomatoes, diced with juice reserved**
1   **3-pound beef chuck roast or beef brisket**

1. Preheat oven to 300°F.
2. Combine beef stock, wine and brandy together in a saucepan.
3. Bring to a boil and cook mixture until it reduces to about 4 cups. Set aside.
4. Meanwhile, heat oil in a large skillet over medium heat. Add sliced onions and sauté over low heat until onions soften, about 10 minutes.
5. Place onions in a large roasting pan or Dutch oven. Add tomato paste and garlic.
6. Drain canned tomatoes, reserving juice, and dice into small pieces. Add tomatoes and juice to onion mixture in roasting pan.
7. Using the same skillet over medium heat, sear beef roast on all sides until well browned.
8. Place meat in roasting pan or Dutch oven on top of onions. Pour beef stock reduction over meat.
9. Wrap pan tightly with foil to seal.
10. Bake for 3 hours or until fork tender.

To serve:

Yankee Pot Roast is best after it has cooled and been refrigerated. When ready to serve, slice Roast and reheat with gravy. Great with Orange Orange Carrots (page 74) and Real Mashed Potatoes (page 70).

57

Sautéed Garden Tomato Pasta

SERVES 4

THIS QUICK PASTA DISH IS BEST PREPARED WITH FRESH VINE-RIPE TOMATOES AND GARDEN-GROWN BASIL.

2	tablespoons salt
1	pound penne pasta
4	cups chopped fresh plum tomatoes
½	cup pure olive oil
3	tablespoons chopped fresh garlic
1	cup sliced green onions
½	chopped fresh basil leaves, additional for garnish
1	cup crumbled feta cheese
1	cup grated parmesan cheese
	salt and pepper to taste

1. Bring a 6-quart or larger pot of water to a boil. Add salt and pasta.
2. Boil uncovered until pasta is al dente, about 6 minutes or according to package directions.
3. Drain and set aside.
4. Chop and seed tomatoes, and set aside.
5. In a large skillet or sauté pan, heat olive oil over medium heat and add garlic. Sauté until garlic is tender. Do not brown garlic.
6. Add tomatoes and green onions. Sauté until onions wilt, about 8 minutes.
7. Add pasta to the skillet and stir to mix well.
8. Add cheeses and continue sautéing until cheeses begin to melt.

To serve:

Season pasta to taste and garnish each portion with several fresh basil leaves. Serve with added parmesan cheese on top if desired.

Agnes says:

A mixed green salad with this entrée rounds off an easy weeknight dinner.

Savory Sides

At Agnes & Muriel's, our list of "vegetables" is long and eclectic, and we like it that way. We call them vegetables, even though only in a Southern restaurant is Macaroni & Cheese considered vegetable enough to make it on such a list.

The Vegetable Plate (a choice of 4 vegetables) is by far the most popular item we serve. We offer everything Mom used to make and more— usually about 18 selections at one time. The appealing list consists of old-fashioned vegetable and side dish favorites, some nutritious twists on old stand-bys and a few traditional dishes from my childhood.

All of our side dishes are vegetarian and all of them are delicious. Enjoy!

Potato Latkes

THE TRICK TO PERFECT POTATO PANCAKES IS IN PREPARING THE POTATOES. IF YOU PURÉE THEM IN A BLENDER, THE LATKES ARE CREAMY AND SOFT. IF YOU SHRED THEM, THEY ARE CRISP BUT LACK BODY. I COMBINE THESE TECHNIQUES; FIRST, I SHRED THE POTATOES IN A FOOD PROCESSOR AND THEN I USE THE STEEL BLADE TO PURÉE THEM SLIGHTLY.

3	large red potatoes, unpeeled
½	cup diced yellow onion
1	egg
1	teaspoon salt
1	teaspoon black pepper
¼	cup vegetable oil, for frying

1. Scrub the potatoes and dry with a paper towel.
2. Cut potatoes into quarters.
3. Shred them in the food processor using the grating blade.
4. Empty potatoes into a large bowl and outfit the processor with steel blade.
5. Add onions to potatoes and return to the processor.
6. Pulse processor several times to further chop the potatoes and onions.
7. Remove potatoes and onions to the bowl, and stir in egg, salt and pepper.
8. Heat oil in a large skillet over medium heat.
9. Ladle ¼ cup of the mixture per Latke into the skillet.
10. Cook until golden, flip and cook other side.

To serve:

Serve immediately, straight from the skillet.

Agnes says:

Potato Latkes are traditionally served with a dollop of sour cream on top and applesauce on the side.

Fried Green Tomatoes

WE SERVE THIS SOUTHERN FAVORITE AS AN APPETIZER WITH RED BELL PEPPER SAUCE (PAGE 79) AND GOAT'S CHEESE CRUMBLED OVER THE TOP. CRISPY AND HOT, THEY ARE ALSO THE MAIN COMPONENT IN OUR VERY POPULAR FRIED GREEN TOMATO BLT AND OUR BIG FRIED GREEN TOMATO "BURGER." THEY ARE, OF COURSE, ALSO A BIG FAVORITE SERVED RIGHT OUT OF THE SKILLET AS A SIDE DISH.

4	medium-sized green tomatoes
$\frac{2}{3}$	cup egg wash (page 4)
1 $\frac{1}{2}$	cups Green Tomato breading (below)
	vegetable or canola oil for frying

1. Slice green tomatoes $\frac{1}{4}$-inch thick and set aside.
2. In a large skillet, heat $\frac{1}{2}$ inch of oil over medium heat.
3. While the oil is heating, dip each slice of tomato into egg wash and then coat each tomato well with breading.
4. Fry each tomato until golden, about 4 minutes per side.

To serve:

Fried Green Tomatoes are best right out of the skillet.

Agnes says:

Every Southern cookbook has a different method for breading and frying green tomatoes. Some use straight cornmeal, others use flour. We combined several recipes for breading. The resulting tomatoes have the cornmeal crunch with an even, crispy coating.

Green Tomato Breading

1	cup Bisquick
1	cup prepared cornbread mix
2	teaspoons celery salt
2	teaspoons black pepper
2	teaspoons granulated garlic

1. In a medium mixing bowl, stir all ingredients together.
2. Dredge tomatoes first in egg wash and then in breading to coat well before frying.

Lemon Sesame Collards

SERVES 8

BECAUSE WE COULD NOT HAVE A TRUE SOUTHERN MENU WITHOUT COLLARD GREENS AND BECAUSE ALL OF THE SIDE DISHES AT AGNES & MURIEL'S ARE VEGETARIAN, I DEVISED THIS RECIPE FOR COLLARDS THAT ARE NOT COOKED FOR HOURS IN THE TRADITIONAL WAY WITH FATBACK. OUR CUSTOMERS RAVE ABOUT THIS SIDE DISH. WE PRECOOK HUGE BATCHES OF COLLARDS DAILY, THEN THEY ARE SAUTÉED TO ORDER.

1	bunch fresh collard greens
1	tablespoon salt
2	tablespoons butter
1	tablespoon sesame seeds
1 or 2	tablespoons freshly squeezed lemon juice
	salt and black pepper to taste

1. Bring a large pot of water to a boil.
2. While water is heating, trim and discard woody stalks from the collards. Cut or tear collards into 2-inch squares.
3. Soak the collards in water to remove any gritty sand. Change the water as needed until the water is clear and collards are clean.
4. Add collards and salt to the boiling water, and boil uncovered for 12 minutes.
5. Drain and set aside. You may boil the collards ahead of time and refrigerate for one day in a covered bowl until needed.
6. Melt butter in a large skillet. Add sesame seeds. Continue cooking over medium heat until the butter and the seeds just begin to brown.
7. Add the collards and lemon juice, and sauté until collards are heated through.
8. Adjust taste to preference with extra lemon juice or salt and pepper.

To serve:

Lemon Sesame Collards are best served piping hot immediately after sautéing.

Aunt Betty's Yeast Rolls

NELLIE WAS LIKE A MOTHER TO ME AND HER SISTER WAS AUNT BETTY. THE TWO OF THEM COULD BAKE UP A STORM AND THEY CERTAINLY TAUGHT ME A THING OR TWO ABOUT BAKING. I STILL LOVE THE RECIPES THEY HANDED DOWN TO ME.

2	packages dry yeast
½	cup warm water (110°F)
8	cups flour
1	3.4-ounce box instant vanilla pudding mix
½	cup sugar
2	teaspoons salt
2	cups additional warm water (110°F)
½	cup vegetable oil
2	eggs, lightly beaten
	nonstick cooking spray
4	tablespoons melted butter

Muriel says:

Rolls can be made through step 9, covered tightly and placed in a zip-top bag in the freezer until ready for second rise and baking.

A good home-cooked meal is not complete without a basket of these warm delights.

1. Dissolve yeast in ½ cup warm water and set aside until foamy.
2. To the bowl of an electric mixer add all ingredients except melted butter. Mix on low speed until thoroughly combined and dough is smooth. It is not necessary to use a bread hook—just use the regular beater on the mixer.
3. Spray another large mixing bowl with nonstick cooking spray.
4. Gather dough in a large ball and set it in the coated mixing bowl. Roll dough several times to coat.
5. Cover mixing bowl with a clean kitchen towel and set aside in a warm, dry spot to rise. This should take about 1 hour.
6. When dough has doubled in size, punch it down, using a fist to literally push the air out of the dough.
7. Spray two small baking dishes with nonstick cooking spray.
8. Pinch off a small amount of dough at a time and roll into 1 ½-inch balls, using palm of hand. Flatten balls and fold over. Pinch together rounded sides and place in baking dish with sides of rolls touching.
9. Brush tops of rolls generously with melted butter.
10. Allow rolls to rise again until doubled in size. About 1 hour.
11. Meanwhile, preheat oven to 350°F.
12. Bake rolls 20-25 minutes or until tops of rolls are golden.

To serve:

Serve rolls with butter and jelly if desired.

Tomato Bread Pudding

SERVES 8

IN THE SUMMER MONTHS, USE HOMEGROWN TOMATOES AND $\frac{1}{4}$ CUP CHOPPED FRESH BASIL
IN PLACE OF THE DRIED BASIL TO MAKE THIS SAVORY PUDDING A SUMMER SENSATION.

2 ½   **cups cubed French bread**
3   **cups coarsely chopped fresh tomatoes, with juice**
⅔   **cup brown sugar**
2   **tablespoons dried thyme**
2   **teaspoons dried oregano**
2   **tablespoons dried basil**
1   **teaspoon salt**
2   **teaspoons black pepper**
6   **tablespoons melted butter**

To serve:

Serve Tomato Bread Pudding
as a side dish alongside
grilled meat or chicken.

1. Preheat oven to 350°F.
2. Butter a 2-quart baking dish and set aside.
3. In a large mixing bowl, toss together bread, tomatoes with juice, brown sugar, herbs, salt and pepper.
4. Pour melted butter over bread mixture and toss gently to coat.
5. Put bread mixture into prepared dish and bake 35-40 minutes or until pudding is set.
6. When done, remove from oven and allow to cool 10 minutes before serving.

Roasted Asparagus

THIS HAS TO BE THE WORLD'S EASIEST ASPARAGUS RECIPE. OUR CUSTOMERS BEG FOR THIS DELICIOUS, NO-FAT VEGETABLE DISH. IT IS ALSO GREAT SERVED COLD ON A COCKTAIL BUFFET WITH A TANGY DIP LIKE THE BUTTERMILK RANCH DRESSING ON PAGE 40.

2   **pounds fresh asparagus**
     nonstick cooking spray
2   **teaspoons seasoned salt or garlic salt**

1. *P*reheat oven to 400°F.
2. Rinse asparagus well.
3. Trim and discard 2 inches or more of woody stalk from the ends of the asparagus, if necessary.
4. Place the asparagus in a single layer on a cookie sheet lined with parchment paper.
5. Spray the asparagus liberally with nonstick cooking spray.
6. Sprinkle seasoning salt over the asparagus. Roll spears around on cookie sheet to coat evenly.
7. Place cookie sheet in oven and roast for 15 minutes or until asparagus begins to brown.

Agnes says:

Serve Roasted Asparagus as a side dish with a drizzling of olive oil and shaved Parmesan cheese. Serve with grilled meats and vegetables for a delicious, light summer meal.

To serve:

Serve warm, cold or at room temperature.

Real Mashed Potatoes

WE USE SMALL RED POTATOES FOR THIS RECIPE. THEY MAKE THE CREAMIEST MASHED POTATOES. AND WE DO NOT PEEL THEM—THE RED SKINS ADD A SLIGHT CRUNCH TO THE TEXTURE. THE BIGGEST SECRET TO SUCCESSFUL, DELICIOUS MASHED POTATOES IS BOILING THE POTATOES IN SALTED WATER. THIS MAKES THE TRUE POTATO FLAVOR POP. FOLLOW THIS RECIPE EXACTLY EVERY TIME AND YOU WILL ALWAYS HAVE PERFECT POTATOES.

2	pounds red potatoes
1	tablespoon salt
4	tablespoons butter
½	cup half-and-half
	salt and black pepper to taste

1. Wash the potato skins well. Do not peel.
2. Cube the potatoes into 2-inch chunks. If the potatoes are too small, they will taste waterlogged after cooking. Do not wash the potatoes after cubing.
3. Bring a 4-quart or larger pot of water to a boil and add 1 tablespoon of salt.
4. Add the potatoes and boil until just tender, about 20 minutes.
5. Drain well.
6. Return potatoes to the warm pot and mash using a potato masher (or a mixer at low speed). If using a mixer, do not overbeat or the potatoes will be gluey.
7. Add the butter and half-and-half, and blend well.
8. Taste and add salt and pepper if desired.

To serve:

Serve Real Mashed Potatoes hot with a little pat of butter on each serving.

Cinnamon Apple Fritters

I HAVE BEEN MAKING THESE FRITTERS FOR YEARS AND SERVE THEM OFTEN WITH GRILLED PORK CHOPS (PAGE 46).

vegetable oil for frying
12 **$\frac{1}{4}$-inch slices Yellow Delicious apples**
$\frac{1}{4}$ **cup flour**
$\frac{1}{4}$ **cup Egg Wash (page 4)**
$\frac{1}{2}$ **cup Bisquick**
1 **recipe Cinnamon Sugar (page 3)**

1. Prepare a deep fryer for frying apples, or heat about $\frac{1}{2}$ inch of oil in a large, heavy skillet.
2. Peel and core each apple and cut into $\frac{1}{4}$-inch slices.
3. Dredge the apple slices in flour and dip each slice into egg wash.
4. Dredge the slices in Bisquick.
5. Place several apples into the hot oil and deep fry, turning once or twice, until golden, about 7 minutes.
6. Roll the fried apples in Cinnamon Sugar to coat thoroughly.

To serve:

Serve piping hot, straight from the skillet. These also make a fine dessert served with vanilla custard or ice cream.

Noodle Kugel

SERVES 12

Noodle Kugel is a traditional Eastern European Jewish side dish. Comfort food at its best, it is similar to a "confused bread pudding" made with wide egg noodles. Every Jewish grandmother has her own special recipe. Some add apples or pineapple, and some prepare it as a savory dish. This is our version made with crunchy roasted pecans and topped with Cinnamon Sugar.

1	pound wide egg noodles
1	tablespoon salt
6	eggs
¾	cup sugar
2	cups sour cream
1	pound cream cheese
8	ounces melted butter
1	tablespoon vanilla extract
¼	teaspoon additional salt
2	cups roasted pecans, chopped coarsely (page 6)
2	tablespoons Cinnamon Sugar (page 3)

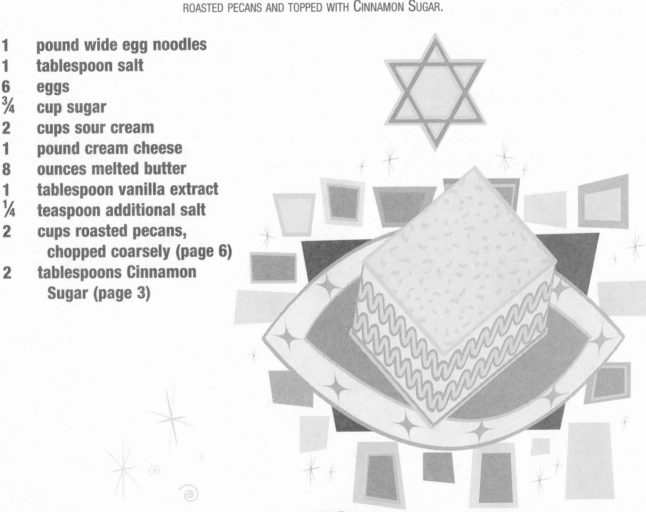

1. $\mathscr{P}$reheat oven to 350°F.
2. Grease a 9 x 13-inch baking pan. Set aside.
3. Bring a 6-quart or larger pot of water to boil.
4. Add noodles and salt to the water. Boil noodles until they are just tender, according to directions on the package.
5. Drain and rinse noodles under cold water. Set aside.
6. Using an electric mixer on low, cream the eggs, sugar, sour cream, cream cheese, melted butter, vanilla and ¼ teaspoon of salt in a large mixing bowl until smooth.
7. Pour cream cheese mixture over noodles and toss well to thoroughly coat noodles.
8. Add roasted pecans and stir well.
9. Pour noodle mixture into the prepared baking pan.
10. Bake at 350°F for 45 minutes or until the center of the Kugel is as firm as the edges.
11. Cool 15 minutes before cutting into 12 portions.

$\mathscr{T}$o serve:

Sprinkle cinnamon sugar over each piece before serving Noodle Kugel warm.

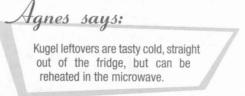

$\mathscr{A}$gnes says:

Kugel leftovers are tasty cold, straight out of the fridge, but can be reheated in the microwave.

Orange Orange Carrots

MY GRANDMOTHER ALWAYS COOKED CARROTS WITH ORANGE SECTIONS. HERE IS MY TAKE ON HER RECIPE.

1	pound carrots
4	tablespoons butter
1	teaspoon salt
4	tablespoons orange juice concentrate
1	Navel orange, peeled, sectioned and seeded

Muriel says:
This recipe reheats beautifully.

1. Peel carrots and cut them into discs, ½-inch thick.
2. Heat a large pot of water to boiling, add carrots and boil until just tender, about 15 minutes.
3. Drain carrots well and immediately return them to the warm pot.
4. Add butter, salt, orange juice concentrate and orange sections to the pot and toss the carrots well to coat.

To serve:
Serve immediately as a side dish.

Sauces, Relishes and Pickles

Sauces, relishes and pickles can turn an ordinary meal into something extraordinary. Anyone can roast a chicken or grill a pork chop. However, when the meat or fish is marinated or served with a zesty sauce or relish alongside, the dish is transformed into a real treat.

The recipes in this chapter epitomize the home cook's resourceful approach to making things taste good. Easy and quick, these relish, sauce and pickle recipes utilize a bountiful harvest or the simplest staples always in the pantry. The key is not to overpower a dish, but to highlight its full natural flavor. Use these recipes to create your own masterpieces—even Muriel would be impressed.

Apricot BBQ Sauce

MAKES 2 ½ CUPS

THIS TANGY, SLIGHTLY SWEET SAUCE IS JUST RIGHT FOR SUNDAY AFTERNOONS WHEN DAD TAKES ON THE BBQ.

1   **cup apricot preserves**
1 ½ **cups freshly squeezed orange juice**
1   **tablespoon freshly squeezed lemon juice**
2   **tablespoons Dijon mustard**
2   **teaspoons Worcestershire sauce**

1. Combine all ingredients in a medium saucepan. Stir to blend.
2. Over medium-low heat, bring mixture just to a boil, stirring often. Cook for 5 minutes while stirring and remove from heat.
3. Pour the mixture into a blender or food processor. Purée until smooth.
4. When ready to use, generously brush on chicken or ribs for grilling or roasting. Baste both sides well several times while cooking.

To serve:

Heat any remaining BBQ Sauce in a small saucepan over low heat until warm. Serve sauce warm in small individual dishes as a dipping accompaniment with the grilled or roasted meat.

Agnes says:

Sauce may be kept in an airtight container in the refrigerator for up to two weeks.

Honey Mustard Dipping Sauce

THIS DIPPING SAUCE ALSO MAKES FOR A DELICIOUS SALAD DRESSING AND CAN BE USED FOR DIPPING ANYTHING FROM FRIED CHICKEN FINGERS TO SWEET POTATO FRIES. IT IS A PERFECT BLEND OF SWEET AND SPICE, AND KIDS LOVE IT.

½ cup honey
¼ cup water
⅓ cup cider vinegar
1 tablespoon plus 1 ½ teaspoons dry mustard
⅓ cup Gulden's brown mustard
1 tablespoon salt
2 cups vegetable oil

1. Place all ingredients except oil in a blender or food processor.
2. Blend until smooth.
3. Very slowly add oil and blend until thoroughly combined and pale golden in color.
4. Chill covered 1 hour before serving.

To serve:

Shake or stir well before serving.

Red Bell Pepper Sauce

MAKES 3 CUPS

THE PERFECT ZESTY FOIL FOR CRISPY FRIED GREEN TOMATOES (PAGE 62). USE YOUR IMAGINATION WHEN PAIRING THIS SAUCE WITH CRISP RAW, STEAMED OR ROASTED VEGGIES, SUCH AS ARTICHOKES, ASPARAGUS OR BROCCOLI.

1	**cup canned roasted red peppers, drained**
2	**cups mayonnaise**
½	**cup extra-virgin olive oil**
¾	**teaspoon celery salt**
¾	**teaspoon black pepper**
1	**tablespoon plus 1 ½ teaspoons Tabasco**
1	**tablespoon plus 1 ½ teaspoons freshly squeezed lemon juice**

1. In a blender or food processor, purée mayonnaise and red peppers until well blended.
2. With blender or processor on, slowly add oil and blend until all the oil is thoroughly combined.
3. Add remaining ingredients and combine well.
4. Chill 1 hour before serving.

To serve:

Stir to make sure ingredients are mixed before serving.

Blender Hollandaise

IN THE 1950S, EVERY BRIDE AND GROOM RECEIVED A BLENDER AS A WEDDING PRESENT. WHEN MURIEL'S WEDDING BLENDER CONKED OUT IN THE '60S AND SHE HAD TO REPLACE IT, I REMEMBER EVERYTHING SHE SERVED FOR MONTHS THEREAFTER WAS PREPARED IN THAT NEW BLENDER. NOW, WHEN I COOK AT HOME, I ACTUALLY USE MY BLENDER ALMOST AS MUCH AS SHE DID.

2   **egg yolks**
1 ½ **tablespoons freshly squeezed lemon juice**
½   **teaspoon salt**
1   **pinch ground cayenne pepper**
1   **cup butter**

1. Place egg yolks, lemon juice, salt and cayenne in a blender.
2. With lid on, blend on medium speed for 15 seconds to combine all ingredients.
3. In a small saucepan, melt butter over low heat until sizzling, but not browned.
4. Turn blender on medium speed and slowly pour the hot butter into egg yolk mixture.
5. Blend 15 seconds more to incorporate butter.

To serve:

This sauce should be served warm as soon as it is made. If need be, slowly reheat any leftover Hollandaise in a double boiler over low heat. Stir sauce often while reheating.

Muriel says:
Hollandaise is delicious served over broccoli, asparagus, and grilled meats and chicken.

Garlic Pepper Jelly

FOR THIS RECIPE, USE RED FINGER PEPPERS OR JALAPEÑO PEPPERS. BE CAREFUL WHEN SEEDING THE PEPPERS—THE VEINS AND SEEDS ARE THE HOTTEST PART.

½	cup seeded and coarsely chopped fresh hot red peppers
½	cup seeded and coarsely chopped fresh hot green peppers
1	medium yellow onion, peeled and coarsely chopped
⅓	cup peeled and coarsely chopped fresh garlic
1 ½	cups white vinegar
5 ½	cups sugar
2	envelopes Certo pectin
6	half-pint glass jars sterilized in boiling water 10 minutes
6	self-sealing lids sterilized in boiling water 10 minutes

Agnes says:

If you have never canned before, this easy recipe is a good place to begin. Most grocery stores now have the canning lids and jars. This makes a great gift, but we bet you will not want to give it away.

1. Place peppers, onions, garlic and half of the vinegar into the bowl of a food processor and process until vegetables are finely chopped but not puréed.

2. Place the pepper mixture in a 4-quart saucepan. Add remaining vinegar and sugar.

3. Over medium heat, bring mixture to a boil and cook for 1 minute.

4. Remove from heat and add pectin, stirring well.

5. Skim foam from top of mixture and discard.

6. Pour into sterilized jars and place lid on jar. Screw band over lid.

7. Wipe outside of jars clean and set jars on a towel to cool completely.

To serve:

This spicy sweet jelly is excellent on a relish tray. It's also a great appetizer. Pour ½ cup Garlic Pepper Jelly over a block of cream cheese. Serve with hearty crackers.

Black Bean Relish

THIS GREAT NO-FAT SIDE DISH IS DELICIOUS WITH GRILLED SEAFOOD OR CHICKEN. WE USE CANNED BLACK BEANS.

2	cups canned black beans, drained
½	cup diced red bell peppers
¼	cup chopped fresh scallion
½	teaspoon ground cumin
½	teaspoon chili powder
1	teaspoon garlic salt
1	tablespoon freshly squeezed lime juice
2	tablespoons chopped fresh cilantro leaves
1	pinch cayenne pepper

1. Rinse the black beans under cold water and drain well.
2. Place black beans in a large mixing bowl and add all remaining ingredients.
3. Gently toss ingredients to mix well.
4. Chill relish at least 2 hours before serving to allow flavors to marry.

To serve:

Black Bean Relish can be served as a cold side dish, or spoon a small amount alongside grilled fish, shrimp or chicken. This recipe is best served within two days of preparing.

Ginger Plum Relish

THIS RELISH IS PARTICULARLY SNAZZY ATOP GRILLED FRESH FISH—ESPECIALLY SEA BASS OR GROUPER.

1	tablespoon finely chopped fresh ginger
1	tablespoon finely chopped fresh cilantro
1	fresh scallion, chopped
3	tablespoons freshly squeezed lime juice
2	tablespoons light brown sugar
1	tablespoon Thai Fish Sauce
1	medium avocado
8	fresh red or purple plums
1	red bell pepper

To serve:

Place small portions of relish on top of and alongside grilled fish.

1. In large mixing bowl, stir together the chopped ginger, cilantro, scallion, lime juice, brown sugar and Thai Fish Sauce. Set aside.
2. Peel the avocado, discard the pit and dice into ½-inch chunks.
3. Pit and dice the plums into ¼-inch pieces.
4. Core and dice the red bell pepper.
5. Add avocado, plum, and red bell pepper pieces to the ginger mixture and toss to coat well. Cover relish and place in refrigerator to chill for at least 1 hour before serving. Any leftover relish may be kept tightly covered in the refrigerator for up to two days.

Summer Ripe Tomato Basil Salsa

SERVES 8 TO 10

2 pounds ripe tomatoes
2 large red bell peppers
¾ cup chopped fresh basil leaves
1 tablespoon salt
1 ½ teaspoons black pepper
1 tablespoon garlic powder
¾ cup pure olive oil
½ cup balsamic vinegar

1. Core the tomatoes with a sharp knife. Cube into 1-inch pieces. Place in a large mixing bowl. Set aside.

2. Cut the red bell peppers into 1 x ¼-inch strips and add to tomatoes.

3. Chop basil and add to tomato mixture.

4. Add remaining ingredients and stir gently to blend.

5. Refrigerate salsa for 1 hour before serving to allow flavors to marry. To maintain its crispy freshness, serve this salad within 2 days of preparing.

To serve:

Serve with Stuffed Portobello Mushrooms (page 18) or as a garnish with grilled chicken or fish.

Muriel says:

Sometimes we toss this mixture with baby lettuces and shaved Parmigiano-Reggiano cheese for a simple salad. It is best made with vine-ripened, sun-kissed summer tomatoes.

Bread & Butter Pickles

Makes about 12 cups

These sweetly sour relish pickles are delicious and will keep in the fridge for weeks.

8	pickling cucumbers
1	large yellow onion, sliced ¼-inch thick and in 1-inch long pieces
½	cup diced green bell pepper
½	cup diced red bell pepper
1	tablespoon salt
2	cups sugar
¾	teaspoon turmeric
¼	teaspoon ground cloves
½	teaspoon celery seed
1 ½	teaspoons yellow mustard seed
2	cups cider vinegar

1. $\mathcal{S}$crub cucumbers well. Trim and discard ends.
2. Slice cucumbers into ¼-inch-thick circles.
3. In a large mixing bowl, combine cucumbers, onion, green pepper, red pepper and salt.
4. Cover with 4 cups of ice and set aside for 3 hours. This crisps the vegetables and removes any bitterness.
5. Drain well.
6. Place all ingredients in a non-aluminum pot or canning kettle.
7. Heat mixture until boiling. Cook until cucumbers just start to lose their bright green color, about 5 minutes.
8. Remove from heat and allow to cool completely.
9. Place pickles in glass jars or non-aluminum containers.
10. Refrigerate until served.

$\mathcal{T}$o serve:

This is great on the relish tray, or served with sandwiches, burgers or even with grilled salmon fillets.

Fire & Ice Relish

ANOTHER GREAT BEFORE-MEAL RELISH OR TOPPING FOR GRILLED FISH.

1	pint cherry tomatoes or sweet grape tomatoes
1	large diced green bell pepper
½	large peeled and diced red onion
¼	cup cider vinegar
1 ½	teaspoons salt
1 ½	teaspoons celery seeds
1 ½	teaspoons yellow mustard seed
2	tablespoons sugar
⅛	teaspoon ground cayenne pepper
⅛	teaspoon black pepper
¼	cup water

1. In a large non-aluminum bowl, combine tomatoes, pepper and onion. Set aside.
2. Combine remaining ingredients in a non-aluminum saucepan. Bring to a boil.
3. Pour hot mixture over tomato mixture.
4. Chill for at least 3 hours or overnight before serving.

To serve:

Serve a small portion of this relish alongside grilled fish.

Muriel says:

Non-aluminum pans and bowls are specified because the vinegar in this recipe might react with aluminum and produce a metallic taste in the relish.

*I*t was during my first cooking job at a resort that I became fascinated with the magic of baking. I carried that passion on to subsequent jobs and ended up working to develop the dessert menu for a group of restaurants in Atlanta that ultimately became known for its fantastic desserts.

I brought that reputation to Agnes & Muriel's, and we too are known for big, scrumptious desserts. In fact, when you walk through the front door at the restaurant, the dessert case is the first thing you'll see: huge bowls of whipped cream next to towering chocolate and Red Velvet cakes, and a stand overflowing with 4 freshly baked pies. We cut the pies into quarters because bigger servings are better for sharing. And all of our layer cakes are 3 tall, oversized layers.

My philosophy is, if a customer is going to splurge on dessert, it might as well be completely indulgent and larger than life—something to really sink even the sweetest tooth into—something that Mom might have made, but just a little bit better.

Aunt Tillie's Honey Balls

MAKES 3 DOZEN

AN EASY CLASSIC, THESE NUTTY SHORTBREAD-LIKE COOKIES ARE DIVINE WITH COFFEE OR A GLASS OF COLD MILK.

½   cup butter, room temperature
2   tablespoons honey
1   teaspoon maple flavoring
1 ½ cups flour
1   pinch salt
½   cup finely ground nuts (pecans or walnuts)
     nonstick cooking spray or parchment paper for cookie sheets
     powdered sugar for dredging cookies

Agnes says:

This recipe freezes beautifully before or after baking.

1. In a large mixing bowl, cream together butter, honey and maple flavoring until pale and fluffy.

2. Slowly add flour and mix until well blended.

3. Stir in salt and nuts.

4. Gather dough into a ball and wrap tightly with plastic wrap. Refrigerate at least 1 hour before baking.

5. Preheat oven to 300°F.

6. Spray cookie sheets with nonstick cooking spray, or line with parchment paper.

7. Pinch off a small amount of dough at a time and roll into 1-inch balls. Place on cookie sheet 1 inch apart.

8. Bake 45-50 minutes. Cookies will darken slightly.

9. Remove cookies from oven and immediately roll each cookie in powdered sugar to coat well.

10. Store any leftover cookies in an airtight container at room temperature.

Brown Sugar Pound Cake

MAKES ONE 10-INCH CAKE

THIS IS TRULY ONE OF THE BEST RECIPES IN OUR COOKBOOK AND THERE IS ABSOLUTELY NOTHING LIKE THIS CAKE SLICED AND TOPPED WITH FRESH STRAWBERRIES AND WHIPPED CREAM. STRAWBERRY SHORTCAKE, AGNES & MURIEL'S STYLE.

3	cups flour
½	teaspoon salt
1	teaspoon baking powder
1	cup solid vegetable shortening
1	stick butter, room temperature
1	pound dark brown sugar
½	cup sugar
5	eggs
1	teaspoon maple flavoring
1	teaspoon vanilla extract
1	cup milk

Agnes says:

To easily grease and flour pans, spray inside of cake pan generously with nonstick cooking spray. Spoon in 2 tablespoons of flour and, tapping pan on palm of hand, coat inside and sides of pan well with flour. Discard any loose flour.

1. Preheat oven to 325°F. Grease and flour a 10-inch tube pan. Set aside.
2. Sift the flour, salt and baking powder together into a large mixing bowl and set aside.
3. Using another very large mixing bowl and an electric mixer, cream solid vegetable shortening, butter, brown sugar and sugar together.
4. Add the eggs one at a time, beating well after each addition. Continue to beat until mixture is fluffy and pale in color.
5. Add maple and vanilla flavorings.
6. With the mixer on low speed, add $\frac{1}{3}$ of the dry ingredients and $\frac{1}{2}$ of the milk to the creamed shortening mixture. Mix just to combine. Turn mixer off and scrape the sides of the bowl well with a rubber spatula.
7. Add $\frac{1}{3}$ of the dry ingredients and the remaining milk. Again, mix just to combine and scrape the sides of the bowl well with a rubber spatula.
8. Add remaining dry ingredients, mix to just to combine. Do not overmix.
9. Pour into prepared pan.
10. Bake at 325°F for 1 hour 20 minutes, or until center of cake tests done when a toothpick is inserted and comes out clean.
11. Allow the cake to cool 30 minutes in the pan on a wire rack. Then, remove the cake from pan and place on rack to cool completely.
12. Store covered at room temperature.

Hudson Valley Apple Pie

AGNES RAISED HER FAMILY IN THE HUDSON RIVER VALLEY. THIS IS HER RECIPE FOR SCRUMPTIOUS APPLE PIE.

1   9-inch piecrust (page 4)

For filling:
¾   cup sugar
1   tablespoon flour
¼   teaspoon salt
2   pounds apples,
       peeled, cored and wedged
1   tablespoon lemon juice
½   teaspoon cinnamon

For topping:
½   cup flour
½   cup sugar
½   teaspoon cinnamon
4   tablespoons butter,
       cut into small pieces

1. *P*reheat oven to 350°F.
2. Line a 9-inch pie pan with piecrust and set aside.
3. Prepare filling: In a large mixing bowl, toss together sugar, flour and salt.
4. Add apples and lemon juice and toss well to coat the apples.
5. Mound apple mixture evenly into unbaked pie shell.
6. Prepare topping: In a small mixing bowl, stir together flour, sugar and cinnamon.
7. With fingers, mix butter pieces into flour mixture until no piece of butter is larger than a pea.
8. Sprinkle topping evenly over apple mixture.
9. Bake on center rack of oven for 1 hour or until juices in center of pie are thick and bubbly. Pie should be golden brown.
10. Remove from oven and cool 1 hour before serving.
11. Store any leftover pie covered at room temperature.

To serve:
Hudson Valley Apple Pie is delicious served warm with vanilla ice cream or fresh whipped cream on top.

Bob's Chocolate Cake with Chocolate Sour Cream Frosting

MAKES ONE 9-INCH THREE-LAYER CAKE

THIS INCREDIBLY CHOCOLATEY CAKE WAS ALWAYS THE FAVORITE DESSERT OF A BOSS OF MINE NAMED BOB.
NOW IT IS ONE OF THE MOST REQUESTED DESSERTS AT AGNES & MURIEL'S. I HAVE BEEN MAKING IT
THIS WAY FOR YEARS AND IT NEVER CEASES TO MAKE NEW FANS.

3	cups flour
2 ½	teaspoons baking soda
¼	teaspoon salt
1	stick plus 3 tablespoons butter, softened
3	cups dark brown sugar
4	eggs
5 ½	ounces unsweetened chocolate
2	teaspoons vanilla extract
1 ⅓	cups sour cream
1 ⅓	cups hot coffee

For chocolate sour cream frosting

3	egg yolks
1 ½	cups sour cream
1 ½	pounds semisweet chocolate

For cake:

1. Preheat oven to 350°F. Grease and flour 3 9-inch cake pans. Set aside.

2. Sift flour, salt and baking powder together into a large mixing bowl and set aside.

3. Melt unsweetened chocolate according to the directions on page 11.

4. In another large mixing bowl, beat butter and brown sugar together with electric mixer until light and creamy.

5. Add eggs one at a time, beating well after each addition. Continue to beat until mixture is fluffy and pale in color.
6. Add melted chocolate and vanilla to butter mixture and mix well.
7. With the mixer on low speed, add $\frac{1}{3}$ of the dry ingredients, then $\frac{1}{2}$ of the sour cream. Mix just to combine. Turn mixer off and scrape the sides of the bowl well with a rubber spatula.
8. Add another $\frac{1}{3}$ of the dry ingredients and the remaining sour cream. Again, mix just to combine and scrape the sides of the bowl well with a rubber spatula.
9. Add remaining dry ingredients, mix just to combine. Do not overmix.
10. Add hot coffee and blend gently but thoroughly.
11. Pour batter evenly into prepared pans. Tap pans on countertop to release any air bubbles.
12. Bake for 30-35 minutes, or until center of cake tests done when a toothpick is inserted and comes out clean.
13. Remove cakes from oven and place pans on a wire rack to cool.
14. When cakes are cool enough to handle, remove them to wire racks to cool completely before frosting.

For chocolate sour cream frosting:
1. In a large mixing bowl, whisk egg yolks and sour cream together.
2. Melt chocolate according to the directions on page 11. Add to the sour cream mixture and whisk until smooth and creamy.
3. Place one layer of cake on plate and cover evenly with frosting. Repeat with other 2 layers and smooth icing over sides of cake.
4. Store any uneaten cake covered in the refrigerator.

To serve:
Sometimes we top slices of this cake with a spoonful of fresh whipped cream and fresh raspberries. It is also great with vanilla ice cream.

Jake Rothschild's Strawberry Buttermilk Ice Cream

MAKES 2 QUARTS

A GOOD FRIEND AND ICE CREAM ENTREPRENEUR SHARED THIS RECIPE SOME YEARS AGO. PERFECT FOR 4TH OF JULY PICNIC.

2	cups heavy whipping cream
2	cups buttermilk
1	cup half-and-half
2	cups sugar
1	teaspoon vanilla extract
1	cup coarsely chopped strawberries
	strawberries for garnish

1. In a large mixing bowl, whisk together cream, buttermilk, half-and-half, sugar and vanilla.
2. Churn in ice cream freezer until mixture is almost frozen but still soft enough to stir.
3. Add strawberries and continue churning until firmly frozen.
4. Remove to an airtight container and store in freezer until ready to serve.

To serve:

Dish up bowls of Strawberry Buttermilk Ice Cream and top with a few strawberries for garnish.

Nellie's Favorite Cake

PASSED DOWN FROM A VERY SPECIAL LADY, THIS EASY RECIPE IS MADE WITH A CAKE MIX AND IS CHOCK-FULL OF FLAVOR.

For the cake layers:

- 2 18 ½-ounce boxes yellow cake mix
- 8 eggs
- 1 ½ cups vegetable oil
- 2 11-ounce cans mandarin oranges with syrup

For the frosting:

- 1 16-ounce container of Cool Whip topping, defrosted
- 2 20-ounce cans crushed pineapple with syrup
- 4 3.4-ounce boxes instant vanilla pudding mix

1. Preheat oven to 350°F.
2. Grease and flour 3 9-inch layer cake pans. Set aside.
3. Combine cake mix, eggs and vegetable oil in a large mixing bowl. Beat well on low speed of electric mixer until light golden in color.
4. Add mandarin oranges and stir gently to combine.
5. Pour into prepared pans and bake 35-40 minutes, or until center of cake tests done when a toothpick is inserted and comes out clean.
6. Cool 30 minutes in pans on a wire rack.
7. Remove cakes from pans to wire racks and allow to completely cool before frosting.

To serve:

Cover carefully and refrigerate cake at least 8 hours or overnight before serving.

For the frosting:

1. In a large mixing bowl, beat Cool Whip topping and vanilla pudding mix on low speed with electric mixer until mixture is light and fluffy.
2. Gently fold pineapple with syrup into frosting mixture.
3. Place one layer of cake on plate and cover evenly with frosting. Repeat with other 2 layers and smooth icing over sides of cake.

Peach Raspberry Cobbler

IF YOU BAKE IT, THEY WILL RAVE.

1   9-inch piecrust (page 4)

For filling:
¾ cup sugar
¼ cup flour
1 pinch salt
2 ½ cups peeled peaches,
      cut into wedges
¾ cup raspberries

For topping:
½ cup flour
½ cup sugar
½ teaspoon cinnamon
4 tablespoons butter, softened, cut into pieces

1. Preheat oven to 375°F.
2. Line a 9-inch pie pan with piecrust. Set aside.
3. To prepare filling: In a large mixing bowl, toss sugar, flour and salt together.
4. Add peaches and raspberries, and gently stir to mix well.
5. Mound filling evenly into pie shell.
6. To prepare topping: In a small mixing bowl, stir together flour, sugar and cinnamon.
7. With fingers, mix butter pieces into flour mixture until no piece of butter is larger than a pea.
8. Sprinkle evenly over pie filling.
9. Bake for 1 hour, or until juices in center of cobbler are bubbly and thickened, and pie is deep golden brown.
10. Remove from oven and allow to cool 1 hour before serving.

To serve:
Serve heaping portions of cobbler topped with vanilla ice cream.

Old-Fashioned Banana Pudding

INSTEAD OF THE TRADITIONAL MERINGUE TOPPING, WE SERVE THIS DESSERT
TOPPED WITH FRESH WHIPPED CREAM AND TOASTED WALNUTS.

1 ¼ cups flour
1 ½ cups sugar
¾ teaspoon salt
1 quart plus 2 cups milk
6 egg yolks, lightly beaten
3 tablespoons butter, softened
1 ½ teaspoons vanilla extract
4 cups vanilla wafer cookies
1 ¼ pounds ripe bananas, sliced ¼-inch thick
1 pint heavy cream, whipped
½ cup toasted walnuts

To serve:
Serve the pudding cold and top each portion with fresh whipped cream and a sprinkling of chopped nuts.

1. In a large mixing bowl, sift the flour, sugar and salt together.
2. Add the milk gradually and stir well, making sure to remove any lumps.
3. Place the mixture in a large saucepan and cook over low heat, stirring often, until just thickened. This may take 10-20 minutes.
4. When mixture begins to thicken, remove from heat and set aside.
5. Place egg yolks in a separate bowl and add 1 cup of the hot mixture while beating well.
6. Return egg mixture to the original hot mixture in saucepan, add butter and vanilla, and whisk until smooth. Set custard aside.
7. In a serving dish, layer vanilla wafers, bananas and custard mixture evenly in 2 layers.
8. Refrigerate until completely chilled.

Lemon Ice Box Pie

MAKES ONE 9-INCH PIE

LUNCH COUNTER DELIGHT. THIS PIE IS JUST SO DARN GOOD I HAD TO INCLUDE IT IN OUR BOOK. I HOPE YOU WILL ENJOY IT AS MUCH AS WE DO.

For crust:

1 ½	cups vanilla wafer crumbs
6	tablespoons butter, melted

For filling:

6	tablespoons butter
⅔	cup freshly squeezed lemon juice
3	egg yolks
1	egg
1 ½	cups sugar

1. **P**reheat oven to 350°F.
2. In a small mixing bowl, stir together vanilla wafer crumbs and melted butter.
3. Pat into a 9-inch pie plate.
4. Bake crust 10 minutes. Remove from oven and set aside.
5. Prepare the filling: In a small saucepan, melt butter and add lemon juice. Set aside.
6. In a large mixing bowl, beat egg yolks, egg and sugar together on high speed for 5 minutes until mixture is very pale and fluffy.
7. Combine lemon juice mixture and egg mixture in a medium saucepan. Heat over low heat, stirring constantly, until mixture thickens and just begins to boil.
8. Remove from heat immediately and set aside to cool completely.
9. When mixture is cool, whip cream until stiff peaks form.
10. Fold whipped cream into lemon mixture. Pour into baked and cooled pie shell.
11. Cover pie with plastic wrap and refrigerate 2 hours or until firm.

To serve:

Serve Lemon Ice Box Pie well chilled.

Strawberries and Cream Cheesecake

MAKES ONE 10-INCH CAKE

THIS CHEESECAKE CAN BE MADE WITH ANY SEASONAL BERRIES—RASPBERRIES, BLUEBERRIES, STRAWBERRIES OR BLACKBERRIES.

For crust:

1   cup graham cracker crumbs
1   stick butter, melted

For filling:

3   pounds cream cheese, softened
2 ¼ cups sugar
6   eggs
2   teaspoons vanilla

For topping:

1 ½ cups sour cream
½   cup brown sugar
2   pints fresh strawberries, rinsed, drained and sliced

1. Preheat oven to 300°F.
2. Line bottom of 10 x 3-inch solid-bottom baking pan with parchment paper.
3. Prepare crust: In a small mixing bowl, combine graham crackers and melted butter together.
4. Pat into bottom of prepared pan.
5. Bake 10 minutes. Remove from oven and set aside.
6. Prepare filling: In a large mixing bowl, beat cream cheese until soft and creamy.
7. Add sugar and continue to beat, scraping down sides of bowl often.
8. Gradually add eggs, beating well after each addition.
9. Add vanilla and beat until just blended.

10. Pour into prepared pan.
11. Place cheesecake pan into a large roasting pan. Fill roasting pan with water to the halfway mark on the side of cheesecake pan.
12. Bake for 3 hours or until cheesecake is as firm in the center as it is along the edges.
13. Remove cake from oven and water bath, and place in the refrigerator to cool for at least 8 hours before removing from the solid-bottom pan.
14. To remove cake from pan, set the cheesecake pan into a larger pan filled with hot water for 10 seconds.
15. Turn the cheesecake pan onto a cookie sheet. Tap the cookie sheet sharply on the countertop until the cake slides out of pan.
16. Prepare topping: Mix together sour cream and brown sugar in a small mixing bowl. Refrigerate until ready to serve.

To serve:

Place a slice of cheesecake on a plate and drizzle sour cream sauce on top. Spoon a generous number of strawberries on top of sauce.

Red Velvet Cake with Cream Cheese Frosting

MAKES ONE 9-INCH THREE-LAYER CAKE

EVERYONE LOVES RED VELVET CAKE. IT IS THE QUINTESSENTIAL VALENTINE'S DAY DESSERT,
OR JUST THE THING TO BAKE WHEN YOU ARE FEELING A LITTLE BLUE.

For cake:

1	cup shortening
3	cups sugar
2	teaspoons vanilla extract
4	eggs
½	cup red food coloring
¼	cup cocoa powder
5	cups flour
2	teaspoons salt
2	cups buttermilk
2	tablespoons white vinegar
2	teaspoons baking soda
	parchment paper

For cream cheese frosting:

1 ½	sticks butter, softened
1	pound cream cheese
6	cups sifted powdered sugar
2	teaspoons vanilla

For cake:

1. Preheat oven to 350°F.
2. Line bottoms of three 9-inch cake pans with parchment paper. Grease and flour pans.
3. In a large mixing bowl, cream together shortening and sugar.
4. Add vanilla and eggs, beating well after each egg.
5. In a small bowl, whisk together food coloring and cocoa, being sure to remove any lumps. Add to shortening mixture and mix well.
6. In another bowl, sift flour and salt.
7. Alternate adding flour and buttermilk to the shortening mixture. End with dry ingredients and mix just to combine. Do not overmix.
8. In measuring cup, whisk vinegar and baking soda together, and immediately add to cake mixture. Stir to incorporate thoroughly.
9. Pour evenly into prepared pans and tap each pan on countertop to remove any air bubbles.
10. Bake 35-40 minutes, or until center of cake tests done when a toothpick inserted in center comes out clean.
11. Remove cakes from oven and set on wire rack to cool.
12. When cakes are cool enough to handle, remove from pans and set on racks to cool completely before frosting.

For frosting:

1. Beat butter and cream cheese with electric mixer until smooth and creamy.
2. Gradually add powdered sugar and then vanilla. Mix well.
3. Place one layer of cake on plate and cover evenly with frosting. Repeat with other 2 layers and smooth icing over sides of cake.

To serve:

Serve Red Velvet Cake immediately, or cover tightly with plastic wrap and refrigerate until ready to serve. Refrigerate any leftover cake.

White Chocolate Bread Pudding with White Chocolate Sauce

A DEFINITE CROWD PLEASER, THIS IS DECADENT AND DECIDEDLY DELICIOUS.

1 pound challah, brioche or other egg bread, cut into ¾-inch cubes
8 ounces white chocolate
6 cups half-and-half
1 cup heavy whipping cream

2 eggs
4 egg yolks
½ cup sugar
1 tablespoon vanilla extract
nonstick cooking spray
White Chocolate Sauce (below)

1. Preheat oven to 250°F.
2. Bake cubed bread for 20 minutes or until dry throughout.
3. Remove from oven and set aside.
4. Increase oven temperature to 350°F.
5. Spray a 9 x 13-inch baking pan with nonstick cooking spray.
6. Melt white chocolate according to the directions on page 11.
7. In a 4-quart saucepan, whisk together half-and-half, cream, eggs, egg yolks and sugar.
8. Place the saucepan over medium heat.
9. Using a candy thermometer, bring the mixture to 180°F.
10. Remove from heat and stir in vanilla.
11. Stir in white chocolate. Mix well.
12. Add bread cubes and stir gently to coat well.
13. Place pudding in prepared pan.
14. Place pudding pan into a large roasting pan. Fill roasting pan with water to the halfway mark on the side of pudding pan.
15. Bake pudding in water bath 45 minutes or until center of pudding is set.
16. Remove from oven and set aside to cool 1 hour before serving.

White Chocolate Sauce

½   **cup half-and-half**
8   **ounces white chocolate cut into ½-inch pieces**
1   **cup heavy cream**

1. Place half-and-half in a medium saucepan over medium-low heat.
2. When half-and-half is just about to boil, remove from heat and stir in white chocolate. Continue to stir until chocolate melts.
3. In a large mixing bowl, whip cream until soft peaks form.
4. Fold whipped cream into white chocolate mixture.
5. Transfer sauce to mixing bowl and cover tightly. Refrigerate sauce until needed.
6. Stir sauce well before serving.

To serve:

Spoon warm White Chocolate Bread Pudding into serving dishes and top with White Chocolate Sauce.

Blueberry Crumble Pie

MAKES ONE 9-INCH PIE, SERVES 6 TO 8

IN THE SUMMERTIME WE USE SWEET FRESH BLUEBERRIES FOR THIS CRUMBLE
AND SERVE HEAPING PORTIONS TOPPED WITH VANILLA ICE CREAM.

1	9-inch unbaked piecrust (page 4)
4	cups fresh or frozen unsweetened blueberries
¾	cup sugar
¼	cup flour
½	teaspoon salt
1	tablespoon freshly squeezed lemon juice
½	cup additional flour
½	cup additional sugar
½	teaspoon cinnamon
4	tablespoons chilled butter, cut into small pieces

Muriel says:

Should any pie be left over, it may
be stored covered at room
temperature for up to three days.

To serve:

Top with vanilla bean ice cream or
freshly whipped cream.

1. Preheat oven to 350° F. Prepare the crust according to recipe and line a 9-inch pie pan with the unbaked crust.

2. Prepare the filling: Pick through blueberries and discard any stems or leaves. Wash and drain well. In a large mixing bowl, stir together the first amounts of sugar and flour with salt. Add lemon juice and blueberries, and gently stir to evenly coat berries. Set aside.

3. Prepare the topping: In a separate mixing bowl, stir together remaining flour and sugar with cinnamon. Using fingers, crumble butter into the mixture until no lump of butter is larger than a pea.

4. Mound blueberry filling evenly into pie crust. Sprinkle crumble mixture over the filling.

5. Place pie pan on a cookie sheet and bake 1 hour 15 minutes, or until the juices in the center of the pie are bubbly and thickened. The crust and crumbs will turn deep, golden brown.

6. Remove pie from oven and set aside to cool at least 1 hour before serving.

$\mathcal{M}$uriel is not much of a morning person. When I was young, she used to call to my brothers, sister and me from her bed, "Make sure you kids get a good hot breakfast before you go off to school." And, completely fending for ourselves, that usually meant a breakfast of champions—toasted Pop-Tarts and a glass of Tang.

Later, when I was a teenager living in vacation heaven—the Catskill Mountains in New York—I got my start cooking in a resort kitchen. Guests from the city would come to take in the fresh mountain air and we would really put on a spread for each of the three meals a day. Today, I call on teenage memories of those early cooking days to inspire the weekend menu at Agnes & Muriel's. We get up early and get a hot breakfast on the table for our customers—so they don't have to.

After all, as Muriel used to say, it is the most important meal of the day.

Catskills Scramble

This is my favorite of our Brunch recipes. The Griddled Buttermilk Pancakes on page 118 come in a close second.

½	cup cream cheese, softened
¼	cup vegetable oil
1	cup caramelized onions (page 3)
1	cup chopped smoked salmon pieces
1	dozen eggs, beaten
1	cup chopped green onions
4	bagels, split and toasted

1. Remove cream cheese from refrigerator at least 30 minutes before preparing this recipe to allow it to soften completely.
2. In a large skillet, heat the oil over medium heat.
3. Add the caramelized onions and smoked salmon, and sauté over medium heat until onions are heated through and smoked salmon lightens in color.
4. Add eggs and green onions to skillet. Stir the mixture well to scramble the eggs and continue cooking until eggs are almost set, about 5 minutes.
5. Add cream cheese and stir well to blend with egg mixture. Remove from heat.

To serve:

Place 2 toasted bagel halves open-faced on each plate. Generously top bagel halves with portions of scrambled eggs. Serve immediately.

Chicken Biscuit Benedict

WHEN A NEW COOK STARTS ON THE LINE AT AGNES & MURIEL'S, WE OFTEN TEASE THEM ABOUT THIS RECIPE . . . THE QUESTION BEING WHICH COMES FIRST, THE CHICKEN OR THE EGG? IN THIS CASE, IT IS THE CHICKEN, THEN THE EGG, AND A HEALTHY TOPPING OF WARM HOLLANDAISE SAUCE. SCRUMPTIOUS!

4	**Grilled Marinated Chicken Breasts (page 55)**
4	**Almost Over the Top Biscuits (page 115)**
1	**tablespoon vinegar**
8	**eggs**
1	**cup Blender Hollandaise, warmed (page 80)**

1. Preheat oven to 300°F.
2. Slice each chicken breast in half and wrap halves in aluminum foil.
3. Slice each biscuit in half and wrap halves in aluminum foil.
4. Place chicken and biscuits in oven to warm while poaching eggs.
5. To poach the eggs, bring a shallow medium-sized pan of water to a slow simmer. Add vinegar.
6. Crack each egg and gently slide egg into the water. Simmer just until the whites are set, but yolks are still runny, about 5 minutes.
7. Remove chicken and biscuits from oven.
8. Place 2 biscuit halves open-faced on each plate.
9. Top each biscuit half with a piece of chicken.
10. Gently lift each poached egg from water with slotted spoon. Drain slightly.
11. Place a poached egg onto each piece of chicken.
12. Ladle Blender Hollandaise onto each poached egg.

To serve:

Garnish each plate with a sprig of parsley and serve immediately.

Almost Over the Top Biscuits

WE ARE KNOWN FOR THE BIG FLUFFY BISCUITS WE SERVE AT AGNES & MURIEL'S AT WEEKEND BRUNCH. NO AMOUNT OF PRODDING FROM MY EDITOR OR PUBLISHER COULD GET ME TO DIVULGE OUR SECRET RECIPE. I JUST CANNOT GIVE IT AWAY— IT'S LIKE A FAMILY HEIRLOOM. MURIEL WOULD NEVER SPEAK TO ME AGAIN IF I PRINTED IT.

This recipe is so very close . . . and I know you will enjoy it just the same.

nonstick cooking spray
4 ⅔ cups cake flour
1 teaspoon salt
2 tablespoons baking powder
2 tablespoons sugar
3 cups heavy whipping cream
1 stick butter, melted
flour for rolling surface

1. Preheat oven to 375°F.
2. Spray a large baking sheet with nonstick cooking spray and set aside.
3. In a large mixing bowl, sift all dry ingredients together.
4. Gently whisk in the cream.
5. Gather dough in a ball and place it on a floured surface.
6. Roll dough to ½-inch thickness.
7. Brush dough with melted butter and fold over in half.
8. Brush dough again with melted butter.
9. Cut into rounds and place on prepared baking sheet.
10. Bake 15 minutes or until the tops of biscuits begin to turn golden brown.

To serve:
Serve Biscuits warm with plenty of butter, jam or jelly and apple butter if desired.

Ronnie's Quiche

SERVES 6

RONNIE IS A DEAR FRIEND OF MINE AND A GREAT COOK. BACK IN THE LATE '70S, WHEN EVERYONE WAS MAKING QUICHE, SHE BAKED A DIFFERENT QUICHE EACH WEEK. WE OFTEN RUN THIS VERSION OF HER CLASSIC AS A SPECIAL FOR WEEKEND BRUNCH.

1	9-inch unbaked piecrust (page 4)
½	cup 1-inch pieces boiled potatoes
¼	cup caramelized onions (page 3)
¼	cup crumbled feta cheese
1	tablespoon chopped fresh dill
½	cup chopped fresh spinach
½	cup shredded mozzarella
1	teaspoon salt
½	teaspoon black pepper
3	eggs
¾	cup heavy whipping cream

1. Preheat oven to 350°F.
2. In a large mixing bowl, toss together the chopped potatoes, caramelized onions, feta cheese, dill, spinach, mozzarella, salt and pepper.
3. Fill the pie shell with potato mixture.
4. In the same mixing bowl, whisk together eggs and heavy cream. Pour egg mixture evenly over potato mixture in pie shell.
5. Bake 1 hour, or until the center of quiche puffs up and the crust is golden brown.

To serve:

The quiche needs to set for a half hour before serving.

Agnes says:

If you do not have time to make your own, frozen or refrigerated piecrust can be purchased in all grocery stores. Be sure to recrimp the edges of a prepared piecrust so it will look homemade.

Country Grits

FOLKS NOT FROM THE SOUTH ARE OFTEN SUSPICIOUS OF GRITS, BUT DOWN HERE WE LOVE THEM. THEY ARE COMFORTING AND QUICK. THIS RECIPE ADDS CREAMED CORN FOR SWEETNESS AND A SHOT OF TABASCO FOR A LITTLE KICK. AT SUPPERTIME, WE TOP THEM WITH OUR LOUISIANA BBQ SHRIMP (PAGE 48).

3 ½ **cups water**
2   **cups heavy whipping cream**
1 ¼ **cups quick grits**
1   **tablespoon plus 1 ½ teaspoons garlic powder**
1 ½ **teaspoons onion powder**
1 ½ **teaspoons salt**
1   **tablespoon Worcestershire sauce**
½   **teaspoon Tabasco**
½   **cup canned cream-style corn**
½   **teaspoon black pepper**
1 ½ **sticks butter, in chunks**

1. Mix water and cream in a large saucepan.
2. Over medium-high heat, bring the mixture to a boil.
3. Add all remaining ingredients, except butter, to the water and cream. Stir well.
4. Continuing to stir, bring mixture back to a slow boil and simmer for 10 minutes or until the grits are tender.
5. Remove from heat and stir butter into grits.

To serve:

Serve Country Grits as a hot side dish with salt and pepper or a little more Tabasco to taste.

Griddled Buttermilk Pancakes

I LOVE THESE PANCAKES. WE SERVE A STACK OF 3 ON A SMALL IRON SKILLET AT BRUNCH AND TOP THEM WITH A SCOOP OF WHIPPED BUTTER AND WARM MAPLE SYRUP.

2   cups flour
1   teaspoon baking soda
2   teaspoons baking powder
2   tablespoons sugar
½   teaspoon salt
2   eggs
2   cups buttermilk
2   tablespoons melted butter
      nonstick cooking spray
      whipped butter
      maple syrup

Agnes says:

Sometimes, we sprinkle ½ cup of chocolate chips, fresh seasonal berries, or roasted nuts (page 6) and a few slices of ripe banana onto the pancake immediately after pouring the batter onto the hot skillet. The possibilities for variations are endless. Use your imagination.

1. In a large mixing bowl, sift together the flour, baking soda, baking powder, sugar and salt. Set aside.

2. In a small mixing bowl, whisk the eggs until beaten. Add buttermilk and melted butter to eggs. Whisk until smooth.

3. Slowly add buttermilk mixture to the flour mixture. Stir just until lumps disappear. Do not over-mix or pancakes will not be light and fluffy.

4. Spray a medium-sized skillet or griddle with cooking spray and heat over medium heat.

5. Ladle ¼ cup of batter per pancake onto the hot surface. When small bubbles cover the top surface of the pancake, turn it over and cook the other side until golden.

6. Remove pancakes to an ovenproof plate. Place the plate in a warm 250°F oven until all the pancakes are cooked.

To serve:
Place 3 pancakes on each plate and top with whipped butter and maple syrup on the side.

Maple Pecan Banana French Toast

SERVES 6

IF YOU SUCCESSFULLY DEVOUR A WHOLE SERVING OF THIS FRENCH TOAST ON A SUNDAY MORNING AT AGNES & MURIEL'S, WE BET YOU'LL HEAD STRAIGHT HOME FOR A NAP. HERE WE HAVE ADJUSTED THE SERVING SIZE SO THE NAP MAY NOT BE NECESSARY.

5	eggs
1	cup milk
1	teaspoon vanilla extract
2	tablespoons vegetable oil
12	slices challah or brioche bread, 1-inch thick
4	ripe bananas
1	cup maple syrup
½	cup roasted pecans (page 6)
2	tablespoons powdered sugar

1. In a large mixing bowl, whisk the eggs, milk and vanilla together. Set aside.

2. Heat oil in a skillet or on a griddle.

3. Dip each slice of bread into egg batter and turn it over to coat well.

4. Place bread on the skillet or griddle and cook until golden brown.

5. Flip to the other side and cook until golden brown.

To serve:

Place two slices of French Toast overlapping onto each plate. Top the French Toast with the sliced bananas, maple syrup and roasted pecans. Sprinkle powdered sugar over each portion.

Muriel says:

We use free-formed loaves of slightly sweet challah or brioche bread that have been braided or twisted for our French Toast. You may use any bread, just remember to slice it 1-inch thick.

Sour Cream Coffee Cake

THIS IS A CLASSIC COFFEE CAKE RECIPE, MOIST AND CRUMBLY AT THE SAME TIME AND FULL OF CRUNCHY SWEET STREUSEL. IT IS WONDERFUL AT BREAKFAST TIME WITH COFFEE, BUT WILL ALSO EASILY PASS FOR DESSERT WHEN TOPPED WITH FRESH WHIPPED CREAM OR VANILLA ICE CREAM.

For streusel:

1 cup chopped nuts (pecans or walnuts)
1 ¼ teaspoons cinnamon
¾ cup sugar

For cake:

3 cups flour
1 ½ teaspoons baking powder
¾ cup butter, softened
¼ cup milk
1 cup sour cream
3 eggs

1. Preheat oven to 350°F.
2. Grease and flour a 9 x 3-inch spring-form cake pan.
3. In a small mixing bowl, stir together ingredients for streusel and set aside.
4. In a large mixing bowl, whisk together flour and baking powder.
5. Stir in softened butter, milk and sour cream.
6. Add eggs and whisk mixture well. Don't worry about any small lumps of butter, they will melt into the cake while it bakes.
7. Pour half of batter into cake pan and top with half of streusel.
8. Pour remaining batter into pan and evenly sprinkle remaining streusel over batter.
9. Bake 1 hour, or until cake tests done when toothpick inserted in center comes out clean.
10. Remove cake to wire rack to cool 1 hour.
11. Remove sides of pan and set on rack to cool completely.

To serve:

Serve cake warm or at room temperature. Cover and store any leftover cake at room temperature.

I N D E X

Almost Over the Top Biscuits, 115

Apricot BBQ Sauce, 77

Aunt Betty's Yeast Rolls, 66

Aunt Tillie's Honey Balls, 91

Baked Potato Soup, 19

Balsamic Dressing, 38

BBQ Baby Back Ribs and
　　Rib Rub, 44

Black Bean Relish, 83

Blender Hollandaise, 80

Blueberry Crumble Pie, 110

Bob's Chocolate Cake with
　　Chocolate Sour Cream
　　Frosting, 96

Bread
　　Almost Over the Top Biscuits,
　　　　115
　　Aunt Betty's Yeast Rolls, 66
　　Maple Pecan Banana French
　　　　Toast, 120
　　Tomato Bread Pudding, 68

White Chocolate Bread
　　Pudding with White
　　Chocolate Sauce, 108

Bread and Butter Pickles, 86

Brown Sugar Pound Cake, 92

Butter, about, 8

Buttermilk Ranch Dressing, 40

Cakes
　　Brown Sugar Pound Cake, 92
　　Bob's Chocolate Cake with
　　　　Chocolate Sour Cream
　　　　Frosting, 96
　　Nellie's Favorite Cake, 99
　　Red Velvet Cake with Cream
　　　　Cheese Frosting, 106
　　Sour Cream Coffee Cake, 121
　　Strawberries and Cream
　　　　Cheesecake, 104

Caramelized Onions, 3

Carmen Miranda Chicken Salad, 30

Catskills Scramble, 113

Chicken
　　Carmen Miranda Chicken
　　　　Salad, 30
　　Chicken Biscuit Benedict, 114
　　Cracked Mustard Seed
　　　　Chicken, 43
　　Grilled Marinated Chicken
　　　　Breasts, 55

Chicken Biscuit Benedict, 114

Chocolate
　　about melting, 11
　　Bob's Chocolate Cake with
　　　　Chocolate Sour Cream
　　　　Frosting, 96
　　White Chocolate Bread
　　　　Pudding with White
　　　　Chocolate Sauce, 108

Cinnamon Apple Fritters, 71

Cinnamon Sugar, 3

Condiments, about, 8

Corn "Fritters," 15

Country Grits, 117

Crab Bisque, 26

INDEX

Crab Cakes, 52

Cracked Mustard Seed Chicken, 43

Cucumber Dill Vichyssoise, 22

Desserts
Aunt Tillie's Honey Balls, 91
Blueberry Crumble Pie, 110
Bob's Chocolate Cake with
    Chocolate Sour Cream
    Frosting, 96
Brown Sugar Pound Cake, 92
Hudson Valley Apple Pie, 94
Jake Rothschild's Strawberry
    Buttermilk Ice Cream, 98
Lemon Ice Box Pie, 102
Nellie's Favorite Cake, 99
Old Fashioned Banana
    Pudding, 101
Peach Raspberry Cobbler, 100
Red Velvet Cake with Cream
    Cheese Frosting, 106
Strawberries and Cream
    Cheesecake, 104
White Chocolate Bread
    Pudding with White
    Chocolate Sauce, 108

Eggs
about, 8
Egg Wash, 4
Catskills Scramble, 113
Chicken Biscuit Benedict, 114
Ronnie's Quiche, 116

Egg Wash, 4

Fire & Ice Relish, 88

Flour, about, 8

Fried Asparagus, 16

Fried Green Tomatoes, 62

Fruits
Apricot BBQ Sauce, 77
Blueberry Crumble Pie, 110
Carmen Miranda Chicken
    Salad, 30
Cinnamon Apple Fritters, 71
Ginger Plum Relish, 84
Hudson Valley Apple Pie, 94
Jake Rothschild's Strawberry
    Buttermilk Ice Cream, 98
Lemon Ice Box Pie, 102
Nellie's Favorite Cake, 99
Old Fashioned Banana
    Pudding, 101
Orange Orange Carrots, 74

Peach Raspberry Cobbler, 100
Strawberries and Cream
    Cheesecake, 104
Watermelon Vidalia Salad, 35

Garlic Pepper Jelly, 82

Ginger, about grating, fresh, 11

Ginger Plum Relish, 84

Green Goddess Dressing, 39

Green Tomato Breading, 63

Griddled Buttermilk Pancakes, 118

Grilled Garlic Broccoli Salad, 32

Grilled Lettuce Caesar Salad with
    Caesar Dressing, 36

Grilled Marinated Chicken
    Breasts, 55

Grilled Pork Chops with
    Cinnamon Apple Fritters, 46

Grilling, about, 7

Herbs and Spices, about, 9

INDEX

Honey Mustard Dipping Sauce, 78

Hudson Valley Apple Pie, 94

Jake Rothschild's Strawberry
    Buttermilk Ice Cream, 98

Lemon Ice Box Pie, 102

Lemon Sesame Collards, 64

Lime Dressing, 31

Louisiana BBQ Shrimp over
    Country Grits, 48

Maple Pecan Banana French
    Toast, 120

Marinated Lamb Chops, 50

Meats
BBQ Baby Back Ribs and Rib
    Rub, 45
Grilled Pork Chops with
    Cinnamon Apple Fritters,
    46
Marinated Lamb Chops, 50
Turkey Meatloaf, 47
Yankee Pot Roast, 56

Michelle's Cabbage Slaw, 29

Nellie's Favorite Cake, 99

Noodle Kugel, 72

Oil, about, 9

Old Fashioned Banana Pudding,
    101

Orange Orange Carrots, 74

Parchment paper, about, 7

Pasta
Sautéed Garden Tomato
    Pasta, 58
Noodle Kugel, 72

Peach Raspberry Cobbler, 100

Peanut Dressing, 31

Peanut Pickled Beets, 34

Pies
Blueberry Crumble Pie, 110
Hudson Valley Apple Pie, 94
Lemon Ice Box Pie, 102
Piecrust, 4

Piecrust, 4

Potato Latkes, 61

Potatoes
Baked Potato Soup, 19
Cucumber Dill Vichyssoise, 22
Potato Latkes, 61
Real Mashed Potatoes, 70
Ronnie's Quiche, 116

Rib Rub, 45

Real Mashed Potatoes, 70

Red Bell Pepper Sauce, 79

Red Velvet Cake with Cream
    Cheese Frosting, 106

Relishes
Black Bean Relish, 83
Ginger Plum Relish, 84
Fire & Ice Relish, 88

Roasted Asparagus, 69

Roasted Elephant Garlic, 20

Roasted Nuts, 6

Ronnie's Quiche, 116

INDEX

Salads
Carmen Miranda Chicken
Salad, 30
Grilled Garlic Broccoli Salad,
32
Grilled Lettuce Caesar Salad
with Caesar Dressing, 36
Michelle's Cabbage Slaw, 29
Peanut Pickled Beets, 34
Watermelon Vidalia Salad, 35

Salad Dressings
Balsamic Dressing, 38
Buttermilk Ranch Dressing, 40
Caesar Salad Dressing, 36
Green Goddess Dressing, 39
Lime Dressing, 31
Peanut Dressing, 31

Salmon Croquettes, 17

Salmon with Cucumber Salsa, 54

Salsa
Cucumber Salsa, with
Salmon, 54
Summer Ripe Tomato Basil
Salsa, 85

Salt, about, 9

Sauces
Apricot BBQ Sauce, 77
Blender Hollandaise, 80
Honey Mustard Dipping
Sauce, 78
Red Bell Pepper Sauce, 79
White Chocolate Sauce, 108

Sautéed Garden Tomato Pasta, 58

Seafood
about, 9
Catskills Scramble, 113
Crab Bisque, 26
Crab Cakes, 52
Louisiana BBQ Shrimp over
Country Grits, 48
Salmon Croquettes, 17
Salmon with Cucumber
Salsa, 54
Smoked Salmon Chowder, 24

Smoked Salmon Chowder, 24

Sour Cream Coffee Cake, 121

Soups
Baked Potato Soup, 19
Crab Bisque, 26
Cucumber Dill Vichyssoise, 22
Smoked Salmon Chowder, 24
Summer Gazpacho, 23

Soy Dijon Marinade, 6

Strawberries and Cream
Cheesecake, 104

Stuffed Portobello Mushrooms, 18

Sugar
about, 10
Cinnamon Sugar, 3

Summer Gazpacho, 23

Summer Ripe Tomato Basil
Salsa, 85

Tomato Bread Pudding, 68

Turkey Meatloaf, 47

Vegetables
Corn "Fritters," 15
Fried Asparagus, 16
Fried Green Tomatoes, 62
Lemon Sesame Collards, 64
Michelle's Cabbage Slaw, 29
Orange Orange Carrots, 74
Peanut Pickled Beets, 34
Potato Latkes, 61
Real Mashed Potatoes, 70
Roasted Asparagus, 69
Roasted Elephant Garlic, 20

INDEX

Stuffed Portobello Mushrooms, 18
Tomato Bread Pudding, 68

Vinegar, about, 10

Watermelon Vidalia Salad, 35

White Chocolate Bread Pudding with
 White Chocolate Sauce, 108

Yankee Pot Roast, 56

NOTES

For chef-owner **Glenn Powell**, the road to Agnes & Muriel's was a long one that began at the tender age of 13 with a job cooking in a resort kitchen in New York's Catskill Mountains. After reaching adulthood, Glenn assumed the position of baker for a large regional restaurant group in Atlanta, Georgia. Then came a promotion to director of menu development, where he spent years developing standardized corporate recipes, and a stint as cofounder of The Festive Feast Catering. In 1995, Glenn said goodbye to the stylized, trendy cuisine of the '80s and '90s, and took a step back in time to open his own restaurant in midtown Atlanta. The concept behind Agnes & Muriel's is to serve classic comfort food, the kind Mom used to make—only with more attitude. Glenn current resides in Atlanta.

INDEX

Honey Mustard Dipping Sauce, 78

Hudson Valley Apple Pie, 94

Jake Rothschild's Strawberry Buttermilk Ice Cream, 98

Lemon Ice Box Pie, 102

Lemon Sesame Collards, 64

Lime Dressing, 31

Louisiana BBQ Shrimp over Country Grits, 48

Maple Pecan Banana French Toast, 120

Marinated Lamb Chops, 50

Meats
BBQ Baby Back Ribs and Rib Rub, 45
Grilled Pork Chops with Cinnamon Apple Fritters, 46
Marinated Lamb Chops, 50
Turkey Meatloaf, 47
Yankee Pot Roast, 56

Michelle's Cabbage Slaw, 29

Nellie's Favorite Cake, 99

Noodle Kugel, 72

Oil, about, 9

Old Fashioned Banana Pudding, 101

Orange Orange Carrots, 74

Parchment paper, about, 7

Pasta
Sautéed Garden Tomato Pasta, 58
Noodle Kugel, 72

Peach Raspberry Cobbler, 100

Peanut Dressing, 31

Peanut Pickled Beets, 34

Pies
Blueberry Crumble Pie, 110
Hudson Valley Apple Pie, 94
Lemon Ice Box Pie, 102
Piecrust, 4

Piecrust, 4

Potato Latkes, 61

Potatoes
Baked Potato Soup, 19
Cucumber Dill Vichyssoise, 22
Potato Latkes, 61
Real Mashed Potatoes, 70
Ronnie's Quiche, 116

Rib Rub, 45

Real Mashed Potatoes, 70

Red Bell Pepper Sauce, 79

Red Velvet Cake with Cream Cheese Frosting, 106

Relishes
Black Bean Relish, 83
Ginger Plum Relish, 84
Fire & Ice Relish, 88

Roasted Asparagus, 69

Roasted Elephant Garlic, 20

Roasted Nuts, 6

Ronnie's Quiche, 116

I N D E X

Salads

Carmen Miranda Chicken
Salad, 30
Grilled Garlic Broccoli Salad,
32
Grilled Lettuce Caesar Salad
with Caesar Dressing, 36
Michelle's Cabbage Slaw, 29
Peanut Pickled Beets, 34
Watermelon Vidalia Salad, 35

Salad Dressings

Balsamic Dressing, 38
Buttermilk Ranch Dressing, 40
Caesar Salad Dressing, 36
Green Goddess Dressing, 39
Lime Dressing, 31
Peanut Dressing, 31

Salmon Croquettes, 17

Salmon with Cucumber Salsa, 54

Salsa

Cucumber Salsa, with
Salmon, 54
Summer Ripe Tomato Basil
Salsa, 85

Salt, about, 9

Sauces

Apricot BBQ Sauce, 77
Blender Hollandaise, 80
Honey Mustard Dipping
Sauce, 78
Red Bell Pepper Sauce, 79
White Chocolate Sauce, 108

Sautéed Garden Tomato Pasta, 58

Seafood

about, 9
Catskills Scramble, 113
Crab Bisque, 26
Crab Cakes, 52
Louisiana BBQ Shrimp over
Country Grits, 48
Salmon Croquettes, 17
Salmon with Cucumber
Salsa, 54
Smoked Salmon Chowder, 24

Smoked Salmon Chowder, 24

Sour Cream Coffee Cake, 121

Soups

Baked Potato Soup, 19
Crab Bisque, 26
Cucumber Dill Vichyssoise, 22
Smoked Salmon Chowder, 24
Summer Gazpacho, 23

Soy Dijon Marinade, 6

Strawberries and Cream
Cheesecake, 104

Stuffed Portobello Mushrooms, 18

Sugar

about, 10
Cinnamon Sugar, 3

Summer Gazpacho, 23

Summer Ripe Tomato Basil
Salsa, 85

Tomato Bread Pudding, 68

Turkey Meatloaf, 47

Vegetables

Corn "Fritters," 15
Fried Asparagus, 16
Fried Green Tomatoes, 62
Lemon Sesame Collards, 64
Michelle's Cabbage Slaw, 29
Orange Orange Carrots, 74
Peanut Pickled Beets, 34
Potato Latkes, 61
Real Mashed Potatoes, 70
Roasted Asparagus, 69
Roasted Elephant Garlic, 20